The

Blood

Magnified

By Linda Musaus

Contents

Introduction

In 1994, it became very clear to me that God was directing me to a practice in the field of natural medicine. Ever since I was a teenager, I have had a strong interest in "medical things" and, because of my own health problems, have read and studied many things concerning the human body, diseases, and pharmaceutical drugs. Through a series of ordained events, I went to Washington, D.C. to a clinic of Integrative Medicine and received training to become certified as a Clinical Nutritional Analyst. This led to further interest in beginning studies toward my degree as a Naturopathic Doctor.

I opened my practice near Savannah, Georgia in May of 1994, and sometime during the summer of 1995, the Holy Spirit began to speak to me about the importance of studying the blood. I was invited to attend the American Naturopathic Medical Association convention in September of 1995, and was excited to hear a fascinating lecture about Blood Chemistry, which confirmed for me the Holy Spirit's direction. It sparked a new excitement in me, and I began to study the blood with greater interest than ever before.

I wasn't exactly sure what the Lord wanted me to do with

my newfound knowledge of the blood, but His direction to study it and my enthusiasm for learning it were unmistakable. My newly gained understanding of blood chemistry, combined with nutritional and metabolic assessments of my clients, greatly increased my ability to help those who came to see me.

When the Holy Spirit gave me definite direction to close my practice in January of 1997, I was confused as to why He would call me to a practice for almost three years and then direct me to close it. However, I knew I had to be obedient to His voice, and with the assurance within me that He must have a better plan, I made the decision to close my practice. Several weeks later, during a long time of prayer, I asked the Lord why I had been led to numerous Scriptures concerning the old and the new covenant. The Holy Spirit spoke clearly and said, "Your **old covenant** with me was your practice, which was born of the **law**; Your **new covenant** with me is your ministry, which is born of the **Spirit!**" I know now that at least some of the knowledge I gained in my practice will be used to help others in my ministry, and that this book is a result of God-directed study of the blood.

The purpose of this book is to give greater insight and revelation to many concerning the power and significance of the Blood of Jesus. In the end, its purpose is to help the believer in availing himself of that power! The evidence of the remarkable power of the Blood is present in our daily lives, but many don't recognize it as such. God formed the Earth and created man with regard to the inherent worth of the Blood of Jesus, knowing what it would mean to mankind. Even in a tiny cell, His plan is evident for all those who would see it! We now know that the human body was created so that its blood flow is essential for physical life, in all men. But at the appointed time in history, the Blood of Jesus was shed, at which point it became "essential" for the salvation and eternal life of all men.

In the beginning, when God created the heavens and the Earth and all the beasts of the Earth, He also had a plan to create a being named "Man" who would be "created in His own image" (Gen.1: 27). Through the revelation of the Holy Spirit, I have come to realize that a large part of that "image" that we as men reflect is the life-giving flow of blood that courses through our veins and is a "type" of the Blood of Jesus. The blood in our natural bodies and the shed Blood of Jesus are inextricably linked, through the design of the Creator Himself!

In the following pages, I have attempted to "magnify" the Blood of Jesus and to show the parallels with the blood of the human body as "magnified" under the scrutiny of the microscope. When we magnify the natural blood under the microscope, we "enlarge it," or cause it to expand. In "magnifying" the Blood of Jesus, we expand its importance, exalt it, make much of it, and esteem it highly, in our minds and in our lives. As a further means of clarification, throughout this book I will refer to the Blood of Jesus with a capital "B," and to the natural blood of the human body with a lower case "b".

As we "magnify" the Blood of Jesus in our lives by causing it to become greater in our thinking, our understanding, and our speech....By esteeming it highly and making much of it .... By speaking what the Bible says about the power of the Blood of Jesus.... By acknowledging that it has the power to deliver, save, cleanse, protect and heal us, we will see much greater victory in our lives! I pray that what follows will be a blessing to the Body of Christ and to the "unbeliever".

CHAPTER ONE

A Historical Perspective

A t the foot of the cross, as Jesus, the Son of God was suffering a tortuous death, were there **any** witnesses present who could have had the spiritual vision to see into the panorama of the future of mankind and understand the immeasurable, eternal importance of the precious Blood that was being shed before their eyes? How many of them were aware that the events that were unfolding had been foretold by the prophets of old, or were they even considering those things at that moment? Did they understand that, at the precise moment of Christ's death, they became the very first benefactors of a new Blood Covenant that would revolutionize not only their own lives, but would transform the lives and the eternal destinies of billions of human beings to come?

When, at the moment of His death, the veil of the temple was torn in two, there was a great earthquake, graves were opened and many were raised from the dead (Matthew 27: 51-53)....wouldn't many have THEN believed He was truly the Son of God?....Yes, but many others still did NOT believe....How could they not have seen the obvious?

Over the centuries, the debate has continued....Was He truly the Son of God, or just a good man, who taught good things? For those of the "scientific" persuasion, those who are only moved by what can be "proven" to them scientifically or "logically," I pose these thought-provoking questions, for the purpose of stimulating introspection.

Are there not only three "logical" conclusions we can come to regarding Jesus? Either (1) He was who He said He was—the Son of God who had come to Earth in the flesh (2) He was a liar, a deceiver and an imposter, or (3) He was mentally ill, or so disillusioned himself that He only **believed** He was the Son of God. In retrospect, if He had been either a liar or a mentally deranged man, how could His teachings have stood the test of time and had such an eternal, life-changing affect on multiplied billions of human beings throughout the centuries? His life and His teachings have been the inspiration of more literary, musical, artistic and dramatic works than those of anyone in history!

How could a teacher or philosopher so great, so influential, have been a fraud? If He **was** just a "good man" or a "good teacher," then how could such a "good" person have lied and deceived so many about who He was? Is it possible, or even logical, that multitudes of people have been so deceived by Him, and yet the entire world uses HIS birthdate as their frame of reference for history? What other man has been so honored and revered throughout history? Certainly not any madman or imposter! Doesn't the test of time reveal the true character of a man? He either was who He said He was, or **everything He said** was a manifestation of a life of deception or insanity. There can be no "middle ground"!

In all of the historical writings concerning Jesus, even works by secular writers of his time, there has never been a record of an act of sin that Jesus committed. For even the "best" of human beings—"good people"—the legacy of a sin-free life would be impossible and inconceivable! So how could Jesus have lived such a life, free of sin, were He not truly the Son of God?

The documentation for the authenticity of the New Testament, which tells the story of Jesus' life and ministry, is well established. There are more than 3,000 different ancient Greek manuscripts containing all or portions of the New Testament that have survived to our time. (1) In addition to the actual Greek manuscripts, there are more than 1,000 copies and fragments of the New Testament in Syrian, Coptic, Armenian, Gothic, and Ethiopic, as well as 8,000 copies of the Latin Vulgate (non-classical Latin). (2) To be skeptical of the 27 documents of the New Testament, and to say they are unreliable, is to totally disregard the facts concerning their authenticity, because there are no documents of the ancient period that are as well attested to bibliographically as those of the New Testament. The small changes and variations from one manuscript to another change no major doctrine….they do not affect Christianity in the least. There are other ancient manuscripts with far less documentation than the New Testament that have never been questioned as to their authenticity!(3)

And how does one explain the fact that there are over 300 recorded prophecies in the Old Testament concerning Jesus, all of which have been fulfilled? Yet these prophecies were written hundreds of years before Jesus came to Earth. What do we do about the eye-witness historical accounts of the death and crucifixion of Jesus, and His miraculous return from the dead? What could it possibly take to convince some people that He truly WAS the Son of God, and that there is saving, cleansing, delivering and healing power in His shed Blood?

Is there **any** other great philosopher or religious leader who can make the claims that Jesus did and offer historical confirmation that He is truly the Son of God, by performing miracles and conquering death? No, not one. Is there any other religion whose "Savior" was willing to die a horrible death to save His disciples from their sin and assure them of life eternal? No, not one. Jesus was not "just" a philosopher or a teacher....He **demonstrated the Truth** of His teachings by **manifesting the results** of that Truth. He **said** He would be raised from the dead on the third day, and **He was,** according to historical record and many eye-witnesses. He **said** He had come to bring deliverance, and His miracles prove that **He did!**

Before His arrest and crucifixion, Jesus was talking with His disciples and was handed a scroll which contained the writings of Isaiah, prophesying Jesus' ministry. Jesus let the people know that, by reading this prophecy of Isaiah concerning Himself, He had come to fulfill it: **"The Spirit of the Lord is on me, because he has anointed me to preach good news to the poor. He has sent me to proclaim freedom for the prisoners and recovery of sight for the blind, to release the oppressed, to proclaim the year of the Lord's favor." (My emphasis)** The Gospels record that He did all of this and more during His ministry on Earth.

Isaiah 53: 4-5 is another passage in the writings of the prophet Isaiah, written 600 to 700 years before the birth of Jesus, which accurately prophesied what the Blood of Jesus would accomplish for humanity:

> "Surely **He has borne our griefs (sicknesses, weaknesses, and distresses) and carried our sorrows and pains [of punishment],** yet we [ignorantly] considered Him stricken, smitten, and afflicted by God [as if with leprosy]. **But He was wounded for our transgressions, He was bruised for our guilt and iniquities; The chastisement**

[needful to obtain] peace and well-being for us was upon Him, and with the stripes [that wounded] Him we are healed and made whole." (Amplified, my emphasis)

This prophetic passage makes it very clear that the suffering Jesus endured on the cross, He endured **to relieve the suffering of mankind!** If we acknowledge that the atonement for **sin** ("transgressions, guilt, and iniquities") was accomplished at Calvary, we cannot ignore the inclusiveness of this prophetic declaration, which clearly embodies **wholeness of body, mind and spirit as part of the atoning work.**

Jesus came to prove that what He also offered was something no other religion offered....the "Good News" of a free gift of salvation and eternal life that was not dependent on a person's works, legalistic or ritualistic asceticism, or sacrifices. Before Jesus' arrest and crucifixion, He had been trying to tell His disciples that they would no longer be slaves to the hundreds of Levitical laws that had kept them in bondage for so many, many years. The "new law," or the "new covenant," would bring them freedom from the captivity of the old law. In the Old Covenant, their righteousness was attained by observing the letter of the law....by making countless offerings to God upon the altar—animal and grain sacrifices—and by attempting to follow the hundreds of written laws, which was humanly impossible.

Whereas in the old covenant (as expressed in the Old Testament), righteousness was attained by observing the letter of the law, Jesus made it clear that mankind could now receive the righteousness of God by the ministry of the Spirit IN us, not by our works or legalism. Galatians 3:13-14 explains it well: "Christ has redeemed us from the curse of the law, having become a curse for us, (for it is written: 'Cursed is everyone who hangs on a tree'), that the blessing of Abraham might come upon the Gentiles in Christ Jesus, that we might receive the promise of the Spirit through faith." Until this point in history, the old covenant of atonement that God had made with Abraham was acknowledged by the sacrificing of bulls, goats, and lambs. But when Jesus' Blood was shed on the cross, He was transfigured into the Lamb of God whose self-sacrifice became the atonement for our sins. In the old covenant, the "mixing" of two peoples' blood was one of the ways they sealed their covenant with each other. Once a blood covenant was formed, it could never be broken. It assured two people that they would always have each others' protection, and that everything they had belonged to each other, **including all their debts**. Historically, the shedding of blood has been an integral part of covenant making and covenant keeping.

In reality, the Blood of Jesus is the "protective seal" of our New Covenant with God the Father! Jesus **cancelled the debt of all our sin** with the shedding of His Blood—and now we owe Him **a debt of faithfulness and submission to His Word, and of living a life that glorifies what He has done for us**. Jesus' Blood was exchanged for our righteousness, and our new Blood Covenant with Him can never be broken! Because of the Blood of Jesus, we have been made heirs of a new and **better** covenant than the old! In comparing Jesus to the high priests of the Old Covenant, Hebrews 8:6 declares: "But now **He [Jesus] has obtained a more excellent ministry, inasmuch as He is also Mediator of a better covenant, which was established on better promises.**" (My emphasis)

One of those "better promises" is that we become "righteous" before God when we **receive by faith** what Jesus has done on the cross, not because we have deserved it by keeping the law. The following passage in Romans tells us that the concept of faith being attributed by God as righteousness is not unrecognized even in the Old Testament (it is "witnessed by the Law and the Prophets"; see also Romans Chapter 4):

"Therefore by the deeds of the law no flesh will be justified in His sight, for by the law is the knowledge of sin. But now the righteousness of God apart from the law is revealed, **being witnessed by the Law and the Prophets, even the righteousness of God, through faith in Jesus Christ, to all and on all who believe.** For there is no difference; for all have sinned and fall short of the glory of God, **being justified freely** by His grace through the redemption that is in Christ Jesus, **whom God set forth as a propitiation by His blood, through faith,** to demonstrate His righteousness, because in His forbearance God had passed over the sins that were previously committed, to demonstrate at the present time His righteousness, **that He might be just and the justifier of the one who has faith in Jesus."** (Rom. 3:20-26, my emphasis)

This passage assures us that God **sees us as righteous**, when we simply receive by faith what Jesus has done **as a propitiation by His Blood!** ("Propitiation" means His "atoning sacrifice"!) However, lest we believe that invoking the power of the Blood of Jesus can become a substitute for righteous and holy **living,** beware! Simply stated, we cannot continue to live worldly and unholy lives and expect to call upon the Blood of Jesus with any real power, because **it is His righteousness within us that seals the power of the Blood**. Because God knows our heart, He also knows the honesty of our **faith**....Therefore, if we **say** we believe, but our lives don't **show it** by honoring what Jesus did, we deceive ourselves (but not God)! If that righteousness is truly **in** us, because we have truly received by faith, we will have the **desire** to live holier lives.

In Romans 7:4:6, Paul gives a wonderful explanation of this truth: "So, my brothers, you also **died to the law through the body of Christ**, that you might belong to another, to him who was raised from the dead, **in order that we might bear fruit to God**. For when we were controlled by the sinful nature, the sinful passions aroused by the law were at work in our bodies, so that we bore fruit for death. **But now, by dying to what once bound us, we have been released from the law so that we serve in the new way of the Spirit, and not in the old way of the written code."** (My emphasis)

Jesus Himself spoke this truth to us in words that even a child could understand: "Whoever has my commands and obeys them, **he is the one who loves me....He who does not love me will not obey my teaching...."**(John 14: 21 and 24, my emphasis) If we truly receive what Jesus did by faith, we will have the desire to obey Him, to live holy lives and to honor Him.

The "New Covenant" by the Blood of Jesus brought to those who would receive it another powerful "better promise"—that of direct personal access to God the Father! In the Old Testament, the access into the "Holy of Holies" in the sacred tabernacle was given only to the High Priest. This was the inner room where the Arc of the Covenant which represented the presence of God was seated. The common man could never enter into it. **But our new "High Priest," Jesus, has given us access to the Mercy Seat of God by means of His shed Blood!** We can now come freely into God's presence through our worship and our intimacy with Him, to ask His forgiveness, to receive His mercy, and to fellowship with Him. We no longer need a human "mediator," because Jesus is now our High Priest, seated at the right hand of God, and the Holy Spirit "intercedes for the saints in accordance with God's will." (Heb.8:1 and Rom. 8:27)

The truth is that it is **only** because of the shed Blood of Jesus that we have personal access to the Mercy Seat of God at any time and in any place. There is no better reason for us to be studying, rejoicing over, teaching, preaching and singing about the Blood of Jesus—and magnifying its importance in our lives!

Jesus' promise to send the Holy Spirit after He Himself left the Earth is another powerful promise of the "better covenant" that the shedding of His Blood brought about. In one reference to the promise of the Holy Spirit, Jesus said "All this I have spoken while still with you. But the Counselor, the Holy Spirit, whom the Father will send in my name, will teach you all things and will remind you of everything I have said to you." (John 14:25-26) This same promise is for us—the Holy Spirit working in our lives to speak to us, direct us, and intercede for us before the Father in Heaven.

In summary, the Word of God makes it clear that we have been the recipients of many benefits of the shed Blood of Jesus....salvation and eternal life....freedom from the bondage of the law and legalism....wholeness of body, mind and spirit....a personal relationship with God the Father and access to the Mercy Seat....righteousness by faith....and the promise of the Holy Spirit to guide us and be our teacher.

So then....what do we make of the Blood of Jesus? Do we "make much of it," or do we deny its power? To deny it is to deny the evidence of what it has done through the centuries....To deny it is to deny **all** that Jesus said, and all that has been said and prophesied about Him....To deny it is to come to the illogical conclusion that He was "just a good man." **The only "logical conclusion" one can come to is that Jesus IS who He said He was....the Son of God....and that His Blood sacrifice was the solution to the sinful, needy condition of mankind! What will it take for you to decide to avail yourself of its power to transform your life?**

CHAPTER TWO

Making Connections

Why Study the Blood Today?

For the past few years, I have had implanted in my spirit an urgency for the people of God to begin to tap into the power and significance of the Blood of Jesus. Over and over I have heard the Spirit say, "Make much of the Blood!" As I was in prayer one day about whether or not to do this teaching, the Holy Spirit answered me: "Yes, it is a very important time for this teaching. My people MUST understand the power of the Blood!"

One reason we must understand its power is that, as the outpouring of God's Spirit becomes greater during these final days before the return of Jesus, Satan's wrath and assignments against the people of God are also going to intensify. We are going to have to use everything within our power to withstand and overcome Satan's plans against us! !

The Blood of Jesus has the power to protect and deliver us from sin and from destruction by Satan, our Enemy! The Word of God tells us that **Satan has already been defeated,** but we must **believe in** the power of the Blood and **call upon** that power in order to receive the benefits of it. Some say that as Christians, we don't have to be fighting Satan all the time, because he's already defeated. However, many Christians obviously need to be freed from the oppression of Satan in certain areas of their lives. I Peter 5:8-9 says, "Be sober, be vigilant; because your adversary the devil walks around like a roaring lion, seeking whom he may devour. **Resist him, steadfast in the faith....**" (My emphasis)

The next verse goes on to say that after we have been through the struggle, God will restore us and make us strong. The Word of God would not warn us to "resist" something that wasn't a threat to us; nor would it tell us to resist something that we didn't have the power and the weaponry to use in the fight! However, many of us have come under too much oppression of Satan for too long because **we have not invoked the power of the Blood!** Many of us know the Word of God, but we haven't taken hold of the revelation that **Jesus defeated Satan with His Blood, and through the shed Blood of Jesus, WE have the same power to defeat Satan!** We must have **faith** in what the Word says about our Blood Covenant, if we are to stand against the attacks of Satan in these last days!

On the other hand, **sometimes what we blame Satan for is in reality a weakness of our own flesh—something we give in to because of our human nature**. We have become a society which is too quick to absolve ourselves of responsibility and to find something or someone other than ourselves to blame! We can't blame the Devil, for example, when we occasionally overeat, or when we give in to temptations of the flesh, such as gossiping. Neither does God ever tempt anyone, for James 1:13-15 says "Let no one say when he is tempted, 'I am tempted by God'; for God cannot be tempted by evil, nor does He Himself tempt anyone. But each one is tempted **when he is drawn away by his own desires and enticed.** Then, when desire has conceived, it gives birth to sin; and sin, when it is full-grown, brings forth death." (My emphasis)

However, we as Christians are never left to our own devices, because the Holy Spirit is there to help us in temptation: "No temptation has overtaken you except such as is common to man; but God is faithful, who will not allow you to be tempted beyond what you are able, but with the temptation will also make the way of escape, that you may be able to bear it." (I Cor.10:13) We must call upon the Holy Spirit and the power of the Blood to help us, and if we do, God promises to deliver us from temptation!

Addictions, compulsions, depression, suicidal tendencies, and generational curses of sickness are all examples of oppression by Satan that require deliverance by the power of the Blood of Jesus and the authority of Jesus' name. They are not things that by our human nature we can easily decide to "resist". As Christians, we must wage warfare against these bondages with all of the weapons at our disposal!

Immorality and worldly temptations of our society seem to be all around us, and our nation appears to be sliding further and further away from the Godly principles on which it was founded. Even the very foundation of God's plan for marriage and the family has been shaken, with the legalization of abortion and gay marriages. In addition to all of the temptations, stresses , and challenges to our lifestyles, at this time in history, a spirit of fear is pervasive throughout the world....Fear of terrorism, fear of persecution, fear of sickness and disease, fear of war, fear of the future....the list goes on. There are probably more fears and more dangers in our world than at any time in history....and the Word of God has forewarned us that this would be so in the last days.

II Timothy 3:1-5 tells us: "But know this, that in the last days perilous times will come: For men will be lovers of themselves, lovers of money, boasters, proud, blasphemers, disobedient to parents, unthankful, unholy, unloving, unforgiving, slanderers, without self-control, brutal, despisers of good, traitors, headstrong, haughty, lovers of pleasure rather than lovers of God, **having a form of godliness but denying its power….**" (My emphasis)

However, verses 14-17 give us **hope**: "But you must continue in the things which you have learned and been assured of, **knowing from whom you have learned them**, and that from childhood you have known the Holy Scriptures, which are able to make you wise for salvation through faith which is in Christ Jesus. **All Scripture is given by inspiration of God, and is profitable for doctrine, for reproof, for correction, for instruction in righteousness, that the man of God may be complete, thoroughly equipped for every good work.**" (My emphasis)

The "good work" that every Christian must equip ourselves for in these last days is to **dispel the darkness for those who are in fear and seeking answers, by ministering the love and mercy of God to them, and by sharing with them the God-inspired Scriptures which will give them HOPE!** One of the most powerful of those Scriptures is found in Revelation 12, verse 11, where John the Revelator saw a vision of Satan being hurled down to Earth and defeated: "**And they overcame him [Satan] by the blood of the Lamb and by the word of their testimony….**" This verse confirms to us that the Blood of Jesus (the Lamb) is sufficient to defeat Satan!! Another Scripture of hope in these last days is found in II Timothy 1:7: "For **God has not given us a spirit of fear,** but of power and of love and of a sound mind." (Both my emphasis)

At this time in history, the relevance of studying the Blood of Jesus is greater than ever before, because there are tremendous, unprecedented challenges present in our world today that are bigger than ever before! God has given us a powerful "weapon"—the Blood of Jesus— to help us overcome those challenges, **but we must put it to work in our**

lives. It has been here for us all along, but too many of us have not recognized it, for one reason or another.

The Water and the Blood Connection

In the following chapters, as we "magnify" human blood and study its characteristics and functions, we will see fascinating parallels with the characteristics of the Blood of Jesus. These parallels can give us revelation into the fact that we are truly "created in His own image." (Genesis 1:27). The Blood of Jesus has been so intricately tied into our very existence and make-up as humans, but the subtleties of our connections with His Blood have seldom been recognized by us as Christians. **The power inherent in the Blood of Jesus was planned and ordained by God "ever since the creation of the world"!**

Romans 1:20 (Amplified) says: "For ever since the creation of the world His invisible nature and attributes, that is, His eternal power and divinity, have been made intelligible and clearly discernable **in and through the things that have been made** (His handiworks). So [men] are without excuse [altogether without any defense or justification]." (My emphasis) This Scripture clearly tells us that we can gain understanding about the invisible, or the Divine nature, by studying things in the natural world.

One of the first comparisons between the spiritual and the natural that the Holy Spirit revealed during the course of my study is related to John 7:38-39, which says: "He who believes in Me, as the Scripture has said, out of his heart will flow rivers of living water. **But this He spoke concerning the Spirit,** whom those believing in Him would receive...." (My emphasis) This Scripture refers to the Holy Spirit as the "living water," and the parallel was made clear:

Natural Water	"Living Water"
--Most common substance on Earth	--Most predominant means of God's communication with us on Earth
--Cleanses	--Purifies and renews
--Sustains life	--Sustains life in Christ
--Makes wet (Quenches natural thirst)	--Covers the "dry places" in our spirit (Quenches spiritual thirst)

These comparisons about water may seem to be unrelated to a study of the blood; however, as you will see, there are numerous connections between the blood and the water, both in the natural world and in the Word of God. Natural blood is composed of 83 % water, so water is an important COMPONENT of blood. Just before Jesus shed His blood, and the Blood Covenant was established, part of His promise to us was that when He left he would send "the Counselor," (John 16:7), meaning the Holy Spirit, who would "guide [us] into all truth" (John 16:13). So the promise of the Holy Spirit, or the "Living Water" being sent to Earth, was an integral COMPONENT of all that God had planned for us in the new Blood Covenant. The "Water" and the Blood were inseparable!

In Luke 22:44, we see water and blood "mixing" again, for it says: "And being in agony, He prayed more earnestly. Then His sweat became like great drops of blood falling down to the ground." His sweat becoming like drops of blood was a "foreshadowing" of the Blood Covenant that had already been ordained since the foundation of the Earth, but which would soon be demonstrated to the world by the physical shedding of Jesus' Blood on the cross.

In the Old Testament, the blood sacrifices of the lambs and other animals on the altar were for the atonement of sins. These sacrifices were a "type and shadow," or a representation of the Lamb of God to come whose Blood atoned not only for our sin, but for everything that comes from

Satan! The blood sacrifices of the Old Testament were brought to the brazen altar, and the brazen laver (a brass basin) was used to cleanse the priests' hands and feet before they entered into the Holy place. Again we see the relationship between blood and water: **the altar represents the Blood of Jesus, and the laver represents the "Living Water," the Holy Spirit**. Both are an intricate part of salvation and sanctification for the believer.

I John 5:6-8 further explains the blood, water and Spirit connection: "**This is He who came by water and blood—** Jesus Christ; not only by water, but by water and blood. And it is the Spirit who bears witness, because the Spirit is truth. For there are three that bear witness in heaven: The Father, the Word, and the Holy Spirit; and these three are one. **And there are three that bear witness on earth: the Spirit, the water, and the blood; and these three agree as one**." (My emphasis)

Jesus came "by water and blood" because **His whole ministry on earth was "witnessed to" by means of His own baptism and death. He was baptized in water** by John the Baptist at the start of His ministry, which was heralded by Heaven opening and the Spirit of God descending on Him. (See Matthew 3: 13-17) The descending of the dove indicated **He was also "baptized" by the anointing of the "Living Water," the Holy Spirit**, to give Him the power to do what He did in His ministry. And **His Blood sacrifice through His death is why He came, which the Holy Spirit has witnessed to ever since!**

When Jesus' side was pierced on the cross, both blood and water flowed out. This was another demonstration of the promise of our righteousness and victory which were to come by His Blood, and the promise of the Holy Spirit (Living Water) abiding in us. His physical suffering assures us that we can have victory over **ours**! One time when I was feeling sorry for myself about all the pain and suffering I've endured in my lifetime, the Holy Spirit showed me a picture of Jesus on the cross, and encouraged me to think of every adverse physical "symptom" I've ever had. As I began to list them mentally, He gently made it clear to me that there was not one symptom I could think of that Jesus had not suffered in much greater magnitude for ME, **so that I could be free from mine**! The power of the Blood and the Living Water working together have sealed it!

We can see another analogy in nature to the healing flow of blood and water that came from Jesus! The Earth is host to many natural healing waters that spring from it. It is truly fascinating that the balance of minerals found in **the composition of seawater is very similar to that of human blood**! The water that comes from natural springs has concentrated levels of sodium, calcium, magnesium, bicarbonate, and sulphur. Bicarbonate spring water has been found to help heal cuts, burns, hardening of the skin, digestive problems, and allergies. Sulphur water has a history of helping arthritis, rheumatism, chronic poisoning, diabetes, skin disease, and urinary disease. (1) What an awesome and wonderful thing it is that all of creation tells of God's love, in that His design in nature so undeniably reflects the benefits of the Blood Covenant He provided! Let's go deeper in examining the incredible connections that God has established between the natural world and that of the spiritual.

CHAPTER 3

Starting With Some Basics

I would like to begin with a discussion of some general facts and considerations about the blood before going into a deeper study of the properties of the blood. Human blood is of great importance clinically, because the analysis of it can reveal much about the condition of the body and give us clues as to what is "missing" nutritionally and metabolically. It tells us a great deal about "wholeness," (or the lack thereof) in the body. A study of the Blood of Jesus and its life-giving characteristics reveals to us how that precious Blood provides wholeness in the body, soul and spirit of the individual, as well as providing wholeness to the Body of Christ, His Church. As this study progresses, you will begin to see how the "components" of Jesus' Blood flow together to assure wholeness.

Why the Color Red?

One of the questions that kept coming up in my spirit when I first began to prepare this teaching was, "Why did God choose to make natural blood the color red?" I felt there had to be a significance to the color red, because I've come to believe that every detail in the Bible is there for a reason, and that God is a God of "details" that have a purpose! Isaiah 1:18 (Amplified) says: "Come now, and let us reason together, says the Lord. Though your sins are like scarlet, they shall be as white as snow; though they are red like crimson, they shall be like wool." In this passage, scarlet is equated with impurity and sin. Scarlet, or red, has always been one of the toughest and strongest of dyes and cannot easily be washed out. In comparing sin with "scarlet," God understood the depth and permanence of our sin, but He also knew that the power in the Blood of Jesus could "wash" our sins and make them "as white as snow."

It makes sense that the permanence of our sin could only be overcome by something more powerful and permanent — the Blood of Jesus! I believe that God made blood the color red as a reminder and a representation of the permanence of our sin which Jesus' Blood overcame. In other words, as Romans 1:20 says, again: "....His eternal power and divinity have been made intelligible and clearly discernable in and through the things that have been made...." (Amplified)

The "Life-line"

In the natural, **the blood is the "life-line" or the "life stream" of the human body.** No part of the body can live without it. And **God's plan was that the body of Christ on Earth would draw its "life" from the precious Blood of His Son.** In the natural, our bodies survive because of the essential flow of the blood to various organs, and the **Body of Christ "survives" and can overcome sin and adversity because of the shed Blood of Jesus!** And just as a transfusion of blood gives **new life** to a person in the natural, the shedding of Jesus' Blood not only assures a person who believes in it a **new life, or a "new birth,"** but it also transforms him into a new person!

Hebrews 9:13-15 confirms this new life by the Blood of the "New Covenant": "For if the blood of bulls and goats and the ashes of a heifer, sprinkling the unclean, sanctifies for the purifying of the flesh, **how much more shall the blood of Christ, who through the eternal Spirit offered Himself without spot to God, cleanse your conscience from dead works to serve the living God?** And for this reason He is the Mediator of the new covenant, by means of death, for the redemption of the transgressions under the first covenant, that those who are called may receive the promise of the eternal inheritance." And II Corinthians 5:17 reiterates hope to those who are "dead in sin": "Therefore, **if anyone is in Christ, he is a new creation**; old things have passed away; behold, all things have become new." (Both my emphasis)

To put it another way, **we can view the blood in our natural bodies as an actual representation of the death and life we receive from Christ!** II Corinthians 4:9-10 says: "We are hard pressed on every side, yet not crushed; we are perplexed, but not in despair; persecuted, but not forsaken; struck down, but not destroyed—**always carrying about in the body the dying of the Lord Jesus, that the life of Jesus also may be manifested in our body.**" (My emphasis) It's manifested in our body **through the blood** because death **and** life both came to us through the Blood of Jesus. The pouring out of Jesus' Blood on the cross – **His death – brought death** to our sin, sickness, and anything else that Satan can do to us; but that same Blood of Jesus also brought new **life** to our body, soul, and spirit! Satan may try his hardest to crush us and put us in despair, but because of the Blood, we can have the victory!

In making another comparison to the natural with regard to seeing Jesus' Blood as the "life-line," we can also think of His Blood as **the "universal donor,"** because **He can "transfuse" the power of His Blood into ANYONE who**

will receive it !! Acts 10:34 says: "Then Peter opened his mouth and said, 'In truth I perceive that **God shows no partiality**. But in every nation **whoever fears Him and works righteousness is accepted by Him**....'"(My emphasis) And once we've received His Blood through salvation, **WE become "universal donors" after HIS type**, because we can then freely give others a revelation concerning all that the Blood of the New Covenant provides for us! If our natural heart does not receive blood flow, it will die — and if non-believers are not brought into the life-giving flow of revelation concerning what Jesus' Blood has done, their hearts will perish for eternity!

Not only is the blood in the natural our "life-line," but the Blood of Jesus is our "life-line" as individuals. The Body of Christ which knows and understands the good news of the work of the cross must recognize its vital role as the "life-line" to the sinner and to the world!! In other words, when we share with others the good news of what the Blood of Jesus has provided, we are literally offering them the promise of a new life here and now, **and** for eternity!

The Blood Has Depth

Microscopic research of blood cells in recent years has given us incredible new insight into the intricate and fascinating components of the cells which can be seen through study of the multiple "layers" of the blood. Scientists can actually look down into the **"depth"** of a drop of blood! State-of-the-art microscopes can now examine living blood factors at up to 18,000 times magnification to determine red and white blood cell activity, immune and nutritional status, hormonal status, and the presence of parasites, yeasts, bacteria, mycoplasmas, and a host of other components.

As I was contemplating how awesome it is that God has given man the knowledge and ability to actually see and study these incredibly minute "inner workings" of the human body, the Holy Spirit again showed me a comparison. He spoke into my spirit that **"Those who want to go deeper into the things of God will get more and more into the 'Blood Flow'!** They will see and experience the 'Divine mysteries'—the **secrets** spoken about in Jeremiah 33:3: 'Call to Me and I will answer you and show you great and mighty things, fenced in and **hidden,** which you do not know (do not distinguish and recognize, have knowledge of and understand).'" (Amplified, my emphasis)

Confused about the exact meaning of "the Blood Flow," I asked the Holy Spirit to define it, and the answer came: **"Being in the 'Blood Flow' is getting into a place of revelation concerning all that the Blood of the New Covenant assures us of!"** As we **delve deeper into the Word,** study it more, and ask for a "spirit of wisdom and revelation"; as we **make a deeper personal commitment to holiness, and to setting ourselves apart for the things of God,** we will experience things we've never experienced before about the **deep** and abiding love of Jesus, and about the **depth** of His commitment to **us.** We must **abide** with Him daily and with His Word in order to enter into those **deep things of the Spirit.**

CHAPTER 4

The "Life is in the Blood"

In magnifying human blood under the microscope, and in studying its properties, we can see that there are functions which the blood performs for the human body that insure the continuation of life....without these functions, there would be no life. In the Old Testament, God spoke to Moses to tell the Israelites: "For **the life of a creature is in the blood**, and I have given it to you to make atonement for yourselves on the altar...." (Levit. 17:11, my emphasis) He was, of course, referring to the blood sacrifices for sin that the Israelites made at that time. Without the New Covenant, for which Jesus shed **His** Blood as the atonement, there would be no life in Christ, no salvation, and no hope for us today. Let's examine some of the properties of the natural blood and contemplate the parallels to the Blood of Jesus.

1. The blood CLEANSES, or transports waste products from the cells to the external environment, mainly by way of the kidneys. The blood "filters out" contaminants from organs so that they can work efficiently. In the spiritual realm, we need to call upon the Blood of Jesus to act as a "filter" to keep out the things of the world that contaminate

our thinking and our living and cause us to be separated from God (or to SIN). I John 1:7 says (Amplified): "But if we [really] are living and walking in the Light, as He [Himself] is in the Light, we have [true, unbroken] fellowship with one another, and **the blood of Jesus Christ His Son cleanses [removes] us from all sin and guilt [keeps us cleansed from sin in all its forms and manifestations].**"(My emphasis)

I believe that God has been giving our nation and the Church a "wake-up call" to start living lives that will glorify Him—to walk in HOLINESS. I used to think that the word "holiness" referred to "perfection," something none of us could ever really achieve. However, God would not tell us to "Be holy, for I am holy" (I Peter 1:16) if it were something we could not achieve. In order for us to walk in holiness and in the power of God, we must first be **cleansed**—and that's what the Blood of Jesus, together with the conviction of the Holy Spirit, does—it **cleanses** us, or purifies us from our sin and shame!

I would often tell my clients that **there is a parallel between cleansing in the natural and cleansing in the spiritual. In natural medicine, cleansing the body of internal toxic materials is considered the essential first step toward regaining one's health**. I witnessed a number of occasions when, during a session of colon hydrotherapy, a person would experience an inner "purging" of the emotions as well, and would begin crying for no apparent reason. God made our bodies so that whatever affects one aspect of our being can't help but affect the others! That is why so many people have recognized that a "wholistic" approach to medicine makes so much sense....because the physical, spiritual, and emotional are so intricately and inextricably related!

In the spiritual realm, **the cleansing by the Blood of Jesus – the washing away of sin and guilt – is the first**

benefit of salvation – and it is also the first step toward "spiritual circumcision"! Circumcision in the natural brings forth a **blood flow**. The "circumcision of our hearts" that Paul talks about in Romans 2:29 means **purifying** our hearts for the purpose of presenting ourselves as holy before God ("But as he who called you is holy, you also be holy in all your conduct."(I Peter 1:15) This "circumcision" helps **bring us into the "Blood Flow,"** because when we "circumcise our hearts," we're getting in right relationship with God and with the Body of Christ.

After we have sought deliverance from sin and temptation, and asked God to forgive us, **we must accept the fact that He has then forgiven us, cleansed us and forgotten our sin.** Many people, even Christians, have a very hard time forgiving themselves, much less fully accepting or believing that God has truly forgiven them. But the Blood atonement of Jesus was **complete**, and **it provided for our peace as well as for our forgiveness of sin.** We will never be at peace until our mind and emotions are free from the bondage of **guilt**!

Isaiah 43:25-26 speaks a powerful word from the vantage point of the Lord our Redeemer: "I, even I, am He **who blots out your transgressions for My own sake; And I will not remember your sins.** Put Me in remembrance; Let us contend together; **State your case, that you may be acquitted.**" (My emphasis) **We are acquitted when we "plead the Blood of Jesus," because we are calling upon Jesus' Blood as our defense. Without the shedding of His Blood, we would have no defense, and we WOULD be left guilty!** This "inner purging" from guilt and shame is essential to the health of our whole being!

2. The blood TRANSPORTS NUTRIENTS by way of the red blood cells. They carry oxygen and food nutrients to every part of the body, which nurture the body to sustain life. In the natural, we must do our part to nurture our bodies

by **taking in** the food. In the spiritual realm, we must **take in our spiritual food**, which is the Word of God, in order to "nurture" the life of God within us!! In the natural, the "dead," processed foods we take in do not adequately supply our bodies with nourishment and energy, because they are NOT what God intended for us to have! It is only when the Word becomes "living" to us that it will sustain us and give us "spiritual energy"!

Every cell in our natural bodies is touched by blood and **nourished by the blood flow.** But our **spiritual "food,"** the Word of God, may not be "touching us" as it should be so that we can be properly "**nourished**" by it. This may happen for different reasons – possibly because we're not "taking in" the Word regularly enough (we may be "starving" ourselves spiritually); or something may be wrong that is causing us to lack revelation or the knowledge of how to USE the Word; or we may lack the faith to believe that the Word of God is the "real thing" and that it is going to WORK for us!

James 1:5 says: "If any of you lacks wisdom, let him ask of God…." and Paul says in Ephesians 1:17 that we can ask for a "spirit of wisdom and revelation in the knowledge of Him." Finally, Romans 10:17 says: "So then faith comes by hearing, and hearing by the word of God." In other words, **the more we feed on the Word, the more it nourishes our faith!**

After being absorbed into the blood, the blood carries, or ACCESSES the food nutrients to the cells of the body, where they are used to produce energy and **new tissue.** The analogy in the spiritual is that the Blood is our ACCESS. The Blood flow of Jesus—His death and suffering—**provided us access** to the Throne of Mercy and to all the benefits of being a child of God. We can now come freely before God to ask for His mercy for ourselves! We now also have access to the "spiritual food" that we need—the Word of God—which the Church Body and our individual bodies use to nurture our **new life** in Christ. The benefits we have accessed through the Blood then change us into a "**new creation**"!

3. The blood contains white blood cells for DEFENSE and REPAIR. They help defend the body against disease, and they act as "policemen" in the blood to recognize and destroy dangerous foreign substances called antigens. Without granulocytes, (one type of white blood cell), infections in the body would spread rapidly. But the Blood of Jesus is sufficient to overcome **any attack** of the Enemy !! The Blood avails for anything Satan tries to come against us with! It is our DEFENSE against danger and destruction! Because I truly have faith to believe that the Blood avails for anything, **I "plead the Blood of Jesus"** every morning and every night over myself, my family and loved ones, my home, my car, and even my finances. When we say "I plead the Blood of Jesus," we are calling upon that Blood as our defense—and recognizing Jesus as our High Priest and Mediator. Without the shedding of His precious Blood, we would have no defense!

The fact that the Blood of Jesus is available to us as a defense—**if we apply it and believe in it**—is incredibly wonderful news! But the truth will make us truly free, for just as the blood in our natural bodies REPAIRS or provides HEALING to the tissues, **the Blood of Jesus is a HEALING FLOW, and His STRIPES BROUGHT the flow!** Isaiah 53:5b says; "....the chastisement [needful to obtain] peace and well-being for us was upon Him, and **with the stripes [that wounded] Him we are healed and made whole.**" (Amplified, my emphasis) The good news is that Jesus' stripes didn't just buy our **physical** health—they brought us WHOLENESS, or healing to every area of our being—body, soul, and spirit!! In the natural, we must have WHOLE blood in our bodies—ALL the components of the blood must be present to do the job!! God desires that **every aspect** of our being comes into wholeness and completeness! The subject of wholeness will be discussed more in the next chapter.

4. The blood carries ANTIBODIES made by the cells of the body to help us fight off infection. Antibodies give the human body IMMUNITY, or resistance, against further attacks from the same antigen. **The Blood of Jesus provides IMMUNITY to the attacks of Satan....it provides us a way of resisting him, fighting him off, and overcoming the effects of his attacks!** I John 5:5-6 says: "Who is he who **overcomes** the world, but he who believes that Jesus is the Son of God? This is He who came by water and blood—Jesus Christ...." (My emphasis)

Again, Revelation 12:11 says: "And they **have overcome (conquered) him by means of the blood of the Lamb and by the utterance of their testimony..**" (Amplified, my emphasis) This Scripture clearly tells us that Satan will be "cast out" (verse 10) because the people of God will overcome him by invoking the **power of the Blood of Jesus and the Word of God!!** The Blood of Jesus is a VITAL, POTENT WEAPON in these last days that MUST BE appropriated over our lives daily to assure our "immunity" against the destructive plans of Satan!!

5. The heart acts as a central pump to CIRCULATE blood throughout the body to various organs. The blood must circulate and GET TO the organs in order to sustain LIFE! Those of us who have the heart and mind of Christ need to be getting around, CIRCULATING, acting as a "life-line" to bring others the good news of the Blood Covenant—and into the revelation of what the Blood has done for us, so that they, too, can have life abundantly—and eternally. There are even those who have been Christians for many years, but who need to hear about the reality of what Jesus' Blood has done for them.

If there has ever been a time in history when people need to be connected to the "Blood Flow," this is the time! This is the "set time" of the Great Harvest of souls that God has ordained before the return of Christ. Our great commission is to be "circulating" the Truth of God's Word! IF we are faithful to do it, Isaiah 55:11 says: "So shall My word be that goes forth out of My mouth: it shall not return to Me void [without producing any effect, useless], but it shall accomplish **that which I please and purpose**, and it shall prosper in the thing for which I sent it." (Amplified, my emphasis) What God purposes and what would please him is for every man to be saved: "[God our Savior], who desires all men to be saved and to come to the knowledge of the truth." (I Timothy 2:4)

The sobering realization of the coming judgments of God should stir up an urgency in the people of God to bring others to a "knowledge of the Truth"….to go into all the world and preach the Good News! Go with me to Isaiah 63:1-6, which speaks of, not a concept of a "spiritual Blood Flow," but a horrifying and REAL bloodshed that is to come upon the Earth.

In this passage, "Edom" represents the enemy of God and His people—a world which will deny Jesus and the Gospel, and whose blood will be shed at Armageddon. Christ will win the victory by Himself, just as He did at the cross. Those who have rejected the Lord will leave Him no other choice but to bring them to terrible destruction when His longsuffering has ended.(1) Most people believe that after the Church has been "raptured" from the Earth, seven years of Tribulation will follow in the Earth, then Christ will return for the Battle at Armageddon, which is referred to as His "Second Coming." This passage is a prophetic picture of what will occur:

"Who is this Who comes from Edom,

with crimson-stained garments from Bozrah [in Edom]?

This One who is glorious in His apparel, striding triumphantly in the greatness of His might?

"It is I, [the One] Who speaks in righteousness [proclaiming vindication], mighty to save!"

Why is your apparel splashed with red, and Your garments like the one who treads in the winepress?

"I have trodden the winepress alone, and of the peoples there was no one with Me. I trod them in My anger and trampled them in My wrath; and **their lifeblood is sprinkled upon My garments**, and I stained all of My raiment.

"For the day of vengeance was in My heart, and My year of redemption [the year of My redeemed] has come.

"And I looked, but there was no one to help; I was amazed and appalled that there was no one to uphold [truth and right]. So my own arm brought Me victory, and My wrath upheld Me.

"I trod down the peoples in My anger and made them drink of the cup of My wrath until they were intoxicated, and **I spilled their lifeblood upon the earth**." (Amplified, my emphasis)

The New Testament also confirms that judgment will come upon the enemies of God who reject the Blood Covenant of Christ. Hebrews 10: 26-27 and 29-30 makes this clear: "For if we sin willfully after we have received the knowledge of the truth, there no longer remains a sacrifice for sins, **but a certain fearful expectation of judgment, and fiery indignation which will devour the adversaries....**Of how much worse punishment, do you suppose, will he be thought worthy who has trampled the Son of God underfoot, **counted the blood of the covenant by which he was sanctified a common thing**, and insulted the Spirit of grace? For we know Him who said, 'Vengeance is Mine, I will repay,' says the Lord. And again, **'The Lord will judge His people.'"** (My emphasis)

Zephaniah 1:17 again speaks prophetically of the day of the Lord's judgment: "And I will bring distress upon men, so that they shall walk like blind men, because they have sinned against the Lord; **their blood shall be poured out like dust....**" (Amplified, my emphasis) These prophecies tell us that a real Blood Flow is coming....**the people of the Earth will either be in the blood flow that leads to death, or the Blood Flow that leads to life**!! They'll either be in the **path of destruction**, or be **kept from destruction**. If you've never been serious about the things of God, it's not too late! We must be at work, "CIRCULATING" the Good News of what the Blood of Jesus has provided!

6. Human blood carries vital HORMONES that keep us in BALANCE. They regulate growth, development, reproduction and metabolism. When hormones are excessive or deficient in our bodies, serious disorders can result, such as diabetes, hypo or hyperthyroidism, and a host of other complications. The Blood Flow of Jesus at the cross was followed by and connected with the flow of the Spirit (Jesus said He was going to send the Holy Spirit after His resurrection and ascension into Heaven, and that is exactly what happened at Pentecost. A "mighty rushing wind" of the Spirit came and fell on everyone present!) So if we have believed and received what Jesus did at the cross when He shed His Blood, **we have also received a flow of the Holy**

Spirit inside of us, and we are much less likely to become "out of balance" in various areas of our lives, or deceived by wrong teaching, because the Spirit **in us** will guide us.

This is not to say that Christians can't and sometimes don't get "unbalanced" in setting their priorities, in their emotions and thought life, and in falling victim to "extremism" or deception in doctrine. The point is, that as Christians, **we must recognize on a daily basis that the atoning work of the cross of Christ gives us power to overcome any "serious disorder" that unbalances our lives!**

We must call upon the power of the Blood of Jesus to cover us **even in our minds and our thought life!** It is sometimes so easy to be taken in by something that looks good, or seems to be "spiritual," or "seems to be from God"! The Word of God in telling about the "signs of the end of the age" says in Mark 13:22: "False Christs (Messiahs) and false prophets will rise and **show signs and [work] miracles to deceive and lead astray, if possible, even the elect** (those God has chosen out for Himself).(Amplified, my emphasis) This is literally taking place in our society today! During the time that I had my practice, I came in contact with "New Age" practitioners who told me of supernatural healings, levitation and other phenomenon being attributed to New Age "healers" and practitioners who are involved in metaphysics.

One of the main "warning signs" we can look for is the claim that these phenomena are occurring because of the self-discipline, "mind training" or other attributes of the practitioner. If **Jesus** is not given the glory and the praise for "miracles," BEWARE !! I John 4:2-3 clearly tells us to "test the spirits": "Beloved, do not believe every spirit, but test the spirits, whether they are of God; because many false prophets have gone out into the world. **By this you know the Spirit of God:** Every spirit that confesses that Jesus Christ has come in the flesh is of God, and every spirit that does not confess that Jesus Christ has come in the flesh is not of God. **And this is the spirit of the Antichrist**, which you have heard was coming...." (My emphasis)

In II Peter 2:1-2, we again hear a warning about false teachers: "But there were also false prophets among the people, even as there will be false teachers among you, who will secretly **bring in destructive heresies,** even denying the Lord who bought them, and bring on themselves swift destruction. And many will follow their destructive ways, and **because of whom the way of truth will be blasphemed."** (My emphasis)

Several years ago, I asked the Holy Spirit to show me how to recognize a "false prophet" or a "false teacher." He spoke into my spirit that **a false prophet or teacher is one who "speaks My Word** and **sounds very good, but speaks it with deception, hypocrisy, or legalism."** He or she may sound very convincing in speaking the Word of God, and that is exactly why we are sometimes deceived! But examining the fruit of a person's life and the way he treats other people is a good indication of his true spirit....in other words, the way he **lives** the Word of God is the true indicator of his genuineness. Matthew 7:15 says "Beware of false prophets, who come to you in sheep's clothing, but inwardly they are ravenous wolves. **You will know them by their fruits....**" (My emphasis)

We must be alert and do everything we can to keep ourselves in the "right balance" and away from wrong teachings and those who pervert the Word of God with their deception! Besides applying the Blood of Jesus on a daily basis—morning and night—to every aspect of our lives—we can and must rely on the Holy Spirit to give us direction in this area. He will help us to "see and know" the things and people which are of God and those that are NOT. When Christians meet someone who gives them a "check" in their spirit—an uneasiness or an "unsettled" spirit—we need to seek the Lord and find out why. It is so important that we not be deceived in these last days—and yet the deception is sometimes very subtle and hard to see. If it weren't, Jesus wouldn't have warned us that **even the elect will be deceived.**

But in I John 2:26-27, we have reassurance that the Holy Spirit in us will help us: "I write this to you with reference to those who would deceive you [seduce and lead you astray]. But as for you, the anointing (the sacred appointment, the unction) which you received from Him abides [permanently] in you; [so] then you have no need that anyone should instruct you. But just as **His anointing teaches you concerning everything and is true and is no falsehood**, so **you must abide** in (live in, never depart from) Him [being rooted in Him, knit to Him], just as [His anointing] has taught you [to do]." (Amplified, my emphasis) Getting deeper into our relationship with God, by abiding in the "secret place" of prayer with Him daily, and taking the time to listen for the voice of the Holy Spirit, will give us greater assurance against deception.

7. The blood's ability to CLOT is one of its most amazing properties! Clotting involves the process of forming a **protective seal** over a cut, scratch, or wound. Clotting is vital to life, because a person would bleed to death even from a small cut if the blood did not coagulate. In the spiritual realm, applying the Blood of Jesus as a **protective seal** against the wounds and abrasions Satan tries to inflict will keep us in physical and mental wholeness! In John 10:10, **Jesus said, "The thief comes only in order to steal and kill and destroy. I came that they may have and enjoy life, and have it in abundance (to the full, till it overflows)."** (Amplified, my emphasis)

The protective seal of the Blood is crucial not only to the spiritual side of our being, but also to the body and soul— our very life in the flesh. Many times Satan attacks even

Christians with negative thinking, reminders of past sin, memories of hurts and abuses, discouragement, depression, insomnia, compulsive behaviors, and sickness in the body. **But, just as with the natural blood, the Blood of Jesus forms a "protective seal" that keeps the wounds of Satan from doing us in!!** Invoking that Blood daily will attest to its power, because Satan knows the power in the Blood of Jesus, and our speaking it will make him flee!

8. The blood carries OXYGEN from the lungs to all parts of the body. Genesis 2:7 says: "And the Lord God formed man of the dust of the ground, and **breathed** into his nostrils the **breath of life**; and man became a living being." (My emphasis) But because of the shedding of Jesus' Blood, the New Blood Covenant **breathes "new life," new hope, and new vitality** into the person who receives it! And when individuals receive it, there is also **new vitality in the "Body of Christ,"** because those individuals bring a new fire and passion to the Body of believers!

I Peter 1:3-4 puts it this way: "Praised (honored, blessed) be the God and Father of our Lord Jesus Christ (the Messiah)! By His boundless mercy **we have been born again to an ever-living hope through the resurrection of Jesus Christ from the dead**, [Born anew] into **an inheritance which is beyond the reach of change and decay [imperishable],** unsullied and unfading, reserved in heaven for you....." (Amplified, my emphasis) This confirms that our Blood Covenant can never be dissolved or reversed – it is eternal! The benefits of it are what give us **hope and abundant life!**

CHAPTER 5

Wholeness Through the Blood

God's Plan: Corporate and Individual Wholeness

The blood in the human body is truly a "living entity"—if you examine it under a microscope, it is literally "teeming with life"! **The components of the natural blood we can also envision as a "microcosm," or a microscopic representation, of the Body of Christ**. The components of natural blood each have a different function, and most of them contribute to the HEALTH of the body. However, there are some components of the blood that may contribute to its unhealthy state, depending upon what's gone wrong or what's "missing" biochemically, nutritionally, or hormonally. Also, **things may enter in from the outside to attack the body through the blood**, such as yeast, parasites, or bacteria.

In the Church, the Body of Christ, we can often see those things that enter in that shouldn't be there, such as false doctrines, religious spirits, competition, envy, gossip, or sin that is "infectious." **These things enter in to attack**

the Body of Christ and make it unhealthy! There are also sometimes "missing" components such as love, forgiveness, nurturing, compassion…. But God wants us to know that His prescription for the HEALTH of the Body of Christ is that we MUST become mature in the things of God. We MUST strive toward HOLINESS and WHOLENESS as individuals. We MUST seek the will and plan of God for our lives and SUBMIT to our calling. And we MUST DIE to ourselves so that the LIFE of Jesus may be revealed in our individual bodies and in the Church Body!! Just imagine what it would be like if we would each do all these things….the Body of Christ would be working as it should….it would be "perfectly and fully developed [with no defects], lacking in nothing."! (James 1:4, Amplified)

When we do these things, we will also see ORDER in the Body. We know from observing nature that God is a God of incredible ORDER! We see order in the blood, in nature's cycles, in the seasons, and throughout the natural world. In the spiritual realm, we know that all things work together in **God's timing**; we read many Biblical references to patience, waiting on God, and the "testing of our faith" over time. Ecclesiastes 3:1 declares that "To everything there is a season, A time for every purpose under heaven…." Many of us are sensing that at this time in history, **God is "setting things in order" for the return of Jesus! That is why He is calling us to holiness, maturity and submission to His plan**….So that we will truly be **ready to become the Bride of Christ!**

In talking about order in the church, Paul says in I Cor. 14:40: "Let all things be done decently and **in order**." (My emphasis) If we are truly "tuned in" to the flow of the Holy Spirit in our corporate worship, we should recognize that the Holy Spirit is NOT going to "interrupt Himself"! The operation of the "spiritual gifts" while "in the flesh" will only bring about confusion, scepticism, and **disorder**—not to mention seriously shutting down the true anointing! That is why we must achieve maturity in the things of the Spirit—learning how to recognize the voice and anointing of the Holy Spirit, and knowing our gifts and callings, so that we then know how we "fit" into the Body. The Holy Spirit KNOWS the perfect order—all we have to do is rely on HIS direction.

God's Word also makes it clear that there is no room in the Body of Christ for competition, envy and strife **which bring disorder in the Body.** James 3:14-16 and 18 says it this way: "But if you have **bitter jealousy (envy) and contention (rivalry, selfish ambition) in your hearts,** do not pride yourselves on it and thus be in defiance of and false to the Truth. This [superficial] wisdom is not such as comes down from above, but is earthly, unspiritual (animal), even devilish (demoniacal). **For wherever there is jealousy (envy) and contention (rivalry and selfish ambition), there will also be confusion (unrest, disharmony, rebellion) and all sorts of evil and vile practices)....**And the harvest of righteousness (**of conformity to God's will in thought and deed) is [the fruit of the seed] sown in peace by those who work for and make peace [in themselves and in others, that peace which means concord, agreement and harmony between individuals, with undisturbedness, in a peaceful mind free from fears and agitating passions and moral conflicts]."** (Amplified, my emphasis)

In further expounding on the "dying of the flesh" which will bring us to maturity, James 4:1-2 presents the challenge for us: **"What leads to strife (discord and feuds and how do conflicts (quarrels and fightings) originate among you? Do they not arise from your sensual desires that are ever warring in your bodily members? You are jealous and covet [what others have] and your desires go unfulfilled...."** (Amplified, my emphasis) The admonition James gives in these passages is that we must desire **HOLINESS and put aside the lusts of the flesh, which include jealousy, competition and envy.** A vital manifestation of that holiness in the Body of Christ will be conformity to God's will for our own life,** and relying on the Holy Spirit to help keep us from the temptation to envy and desire **others' gifts, talents, "positions," and calling to ministry. When individuals in the Body of Christ mature to the point of desiring and submitting ONLY to God's plan and will for their own life, we will truly begin to see GODLY ORDER come into the Church!!**

When looking at the blood in the natural, we know that everything—the cells, hormones, oxygen, pH, antibodies—must be in ORDER or balance for everything to work as it should. So we see the parallel between the "microcosm" of the blood and the Body of Christ: EVERYTHING MUST BE IN ORDER, and God has laid out for us the perfect order of things in both!! In the Body of Christ, the Word of God and the Holy Spirit give us our guidelines for order!!

A few years ago, the Holy Spirit spoke clearly to me about the subject of wholeness in the Body of Christ: "**We are all ONE in Christ through the Blood of Christ**. We're all redeemed by the same Blood—we all came from Adam. We all have the same blood "type" if we're believers—Jesus' Blood type!! There IS NO black or white or red or yellow in the Kingdom of God—there is only **wholeness through the Blood** for each individual, which brings wholeness to the Body of Christ!"

When we in the Church begin to get a revelation of the power of the Blood that is available to us as a **corporate body**, and begin to nurture a feeling of ONENESS within the Body, we will see a much greater outpouring of the Holy Spirit and of power among us! The power that can also come from consistent **corporate prayer** cannot be underestimated! Meditate on this powerful Scripture and receive a fresh revelation: "Again I tell you, if two of you on earth agree (harmonize together, make a symphony together) about whatever [anything and everything] they may ask, it will come to pass and be done for them by my Father in heaven. For wherever two or three are gathered (drawn together as my followers) in (into) My name, **there I AM in the midst of them**." (Matt. 18:19-20, Amplified, my emphasis) What an amazing promise!

Most churches today do not come together for times of corporate prayer or meet solely for the purpose of praying. I firmly believe that many churches today would not be in strife, separation and decline if they would only come together and pray—**the corporate anointing would destroy yokes of bondage**, bring the church members into oneness with each other, and make the Enemy flee!

In the days ahead, as God's true "prayer warriors," His intercessors, persist in invoking Heaven for a mighty move of God such as we've never seen on Earth, I believe we will see denominational "walls" come down. The result will be a "oneness" in the Church Body such as the Earth has never seen! By this, I am referring to a **oneness of the Spirit, reflecting mutual love for one another and a common desire to see the purposes of God fulfilled.** This "oneness" will, in turn, evoke a power from the corporate Body that will manifest itself in unprecedented "signs, wonders, and miracles." This will cause the wrath of Satan to become greater against the people of God, but our protection will be our ability to "overcome him by the Blood of the Lamb and the word of our testimony." If it will work for us as individuals, (and the Word of God says it will), then how much more powerful will it be when we are invoking the Blood corporately?

Rx for Biblical Wholeness

In order for us to move toward true wholeness in the Body, we must first become mature individually in the things of God. Recently, as I was praying about the teaching concerning "wholeness," the Holy Spirit directed me to look up Hebrews 5:7-10. As I read the passage, I suddenly realized that this Scripture explains the process by which Jesus Himself came into wholeness: "In the days of His flesh [Jesus] offered up definite, special petitions [for that which He not only wanted but needed] and supplications with strong crying and tears to Him Who was [always] able to save Him [out] from death, and He was heard **because of His reverence toward God** [His godly fear, His piety, in that He shrank from the horrors of separation from the bright presence of the Father]. Although He was a Son, **He learned** [active, special] **obedience** through what He suffered and, **[His completed experience] making Him perfectly [equipped]**, He became the Author and Source of eternal salvation to all those who give heed and obey Him, being designated and recognized and saluted by God as High Priest after the order (with the rank) of Melchizedek." (Amplified, my emphasis)

Even Jesus had to learn obedience and reverent submission to God His Father, and He learned it through His suffering and humiliation. For Jesus, **this was not a matter of having to overcome the sin of disobedience,** because He had no sin in Him. For Him, it was a matter of **growing and maturing in obedience**....in other words, He grew from one aspect to another in His **measure** of obedience to God, as He overcame the "human" condition of suffering. This is the same concept expressed in Luke 2:52, which states, "And Jesus **increased in wisdom and stature, and in favor with God and men.**" (My emphasis) The result of all of His growth and "increase" was **perfection**.

The following two passages show us that **Jesus had a**

will independent of His deity! Philippians 2:7-8 says "….[He] **made Himself** of no reputation, taking the form of a bondservant, and coming in the likeness of men. And being found in appearance as a man, He humbled Himself and became obedient to the point of death, even the death of the cross." (My emphasis) And John 10:17-18 is powerful: "For this [reason] the Father loves Me, because I lay down My [own] life—to take it back again. **No one takes it away from Me. On the contrary, I lay it down voluntarily.** [I put it from Myself.] I am authorized and have power to lay it down (to resign it) and I am authorized and have power to take it back again. These are the instructions (orders) which I have received [as My charge] from My Father." (Amplified, my emphasis)

Jesus submitted His will to the will of God for His life and **obeyed**, and **only then** did His completed experience make Him **wholly and perfectly equipped** to become the High Priest for us all! His complete submission to the will of God is what brought Him into wholeness and into His prophetic destiny in God! These passages are a clear example to us, for **none of us will ever be completely WHOLE until our mind, will and emotions (the "soul" part of our being), are submitted to the will and plan of God for our lives**! No matter what we are doing, or what we think we are "doing for God," it will never completely satisfy us unless it is within the sovereign plan of God for our lives.

The Holy Spirit revealed this in an intriguing comparison which points out, once again, how we can look at striking parallels between the spiritual and the natural which reflect the incredible perfection of God's order. The maturation process of a red blood cell is a complex biochemical process regulated by numerous agents. One of the main agents is an "intrinsic factor," which is produced by the stomach. The intrinsic factor complexes with an "extrinsic factor," which is Vitamin B-12. The combining of these two factors is responsible for the absorption of the intrinsic factor from the intestinal tract into the blood, where the cell comes into maturity. (1) While reviewing this information, **I suddenly saw this clear parallel between the maturing of a red blood cell and the process of an individual's maturing in Christ:**

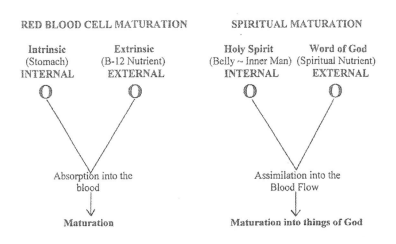

RED BLOOD CELL MATURATION   SPIRITUAL MATURATION

Intrinsic	Extrinsic	Holy Spirit	Word of God
(Stomach)	(B-12 Nutrient)	(Belly ~ Inner Man)	(Spiritual Nutrient)
INTERNAL	EXTERNAL	INTERNAL	EXTERNAL

Absorption into the blood   Assimilation into the Blood Flow

Maturation   Maturation into things of God

The Holy Spirit is our Counselor, our Guide, and our Teacher. **The more we communicate with Him and learn to hear His voice, the more we strengthen the "inner man."** When we add to this relationship the consistent "taking in" of spiritual nourishment through the uncompromised Word of God, we WILL go "deeper" into the things of God. We will also enter into a deeper revelation of the power and significance of the Blood of Jesus, or get more into the "Blood Flow." As we do these things, **we can't help but become more mature in our walk with God (and in our relationships with others in the Body of Christ!)**

God is implanting an urgency in many Christians right now to seek after and fulfill the destiny He has for their lives. The fields are ripe for harvest and the Kingdom's work must be done! God cares so much about us that He wants us to experience not only wholeness, but the "abundant life" that results from it, because the peace of God will reign in our lives when we are in the center of His will!

The more I have studied and contemplated all the ramifications of Isaiah 53:5, the more I am convinced of this: that God's plan for us was **not just for** eternal salvation, forgiveness of sin and physical healing, but that His desire for us was that we live in **wholeness of body, soul and spirit.** The Amplified version makes this so very clear: "But He was wounded for our transgressions, He was bruised for our **guilt and iniquities**; the chastisement [needful to obtain] **peace and well-being** for us was upon Him, and with the stripes [that wounded] Him **we are healed and made whole.**" (My emphasis) The condition of **wholeness** is not simply a "warm, fuzzy feeling" we arrive at concerning ourselves or our accomplishments in life—**it is the sum total of all of God's plans, purposes and desires for us that comprise the "abundant life"!!**

I believe that the reason many people lose the battle over their problem or fail to receive their healing and wholeness is that they become weary in waiting, and they "give up" on the promise of God when He doesn't answer their prayer when they think He should. The bottom line is that **the Blood of Jesus provided the atonement for our wholeness**—physical, spiritual, mental and emotional health! We must be willing to submit to God's plan (as Jesus Himself did!) to see the promise of God come about in our lives….and we must realize that the plan will be different for each individual!

Hebrews 10:35-36 expresses this in a wonderful way for those of us who are seeking His plan but feel that we're still wandering in the wilderness: "Do not, therefore, fling away your fearless confidence, for it carries a great and glorious compensation of reward. **For you have need of steadfast**

patience and endurance, so that you may perform and fully accomplish the will of God, and thus receive and carry away [and enjoy to the full] what is promised." (Amplified, my emphasis)

During the time I was in practice, I received a prophetic word which said that a large part of my ministry would be teaching. At the time, I believed that the practice I was in was God's plan and that I would be doing it until He returned. Also, I considered that I WAS already teaching, since I was instructing my clients on how to take better care of themselves, and I was teaching seminars and other classes. After I closed my practice with definite direction from the Lord, I remembered the prophecy and asked Him one day, "Lord, you said my ministry would be teaching. What is it you want me to teach?" The immediate answer came back loud and clear: "I want you to teach about wholeness." My reply was: "Lord, if you want me to teach about **your** idea of wholeness, you're going to have to teach ME!!"

When we pray with a submitted heart and with the right motivation, The Holy Spirit will give us all we need to do the job He's asked us to do. The result of my prayer was that the Holy Spirit began to speak to me over the next three days many things about wholeness and healing that I had never heard before. The Word of God tells us that in the latter days, knowledge will increase. I don't believe that the increase is only referring to technology, but I believe God meant that an increase would come in all fields of knowledge, both in the natural and in the spiritual. At this time in history, God is revealing Himself to His people in deeper, more intimate, and more extraordinary ways than ever before!

As humans, we are really a three-dimensional being: body, soul, and spirit. In order for us to be truly WHOLE, all three dimensions must line up with what the Word says is

God's plan for us! When we receive Jesus as our Redeemer, Lord and Savior, our "spirit" man comes into wholeness—the union with the Holy Spirit completes it. Our "spirit man" is the part of us that seeks to be like God and to have right relationship with Him—to "image" after Him. As Colossians 3:9-10 says: "....you have put off the old man with his deeds, and have put on the new man, who is renewed in knowledge **according to the image of Him who created him....**" (My emphasis) Our spirit is continually renewed through the knowledge of the Word of our Creator!

None of us wants to suffer in our physical bodies, and many of us gladly claim the promise of physical healing in Isaiah 53. But verse 5 also states that "the chastisement [needful to obtain] peace and well-being for us was upon Him...."(Amplified) This part refers to the wholeness in the realm of the soul that is a part of Jesus' redemptive work on the cross. The soul encompasses the mind, will and emotions of the individual. In order for someone to have true peace, the healthy state of the mind and emotions is probably even more crucial than the physical well being. And as we just saw, the realm of the soul that governs the "will" does not come into **complete** peace or wholeness until it is submitted to the will of God for a person's life.

God knew when He created us that as human beings, we would naturally want the blessings that are described in God's Word, but He also knew that not many would be willing to make the sacrifice of commitment that demands doing OUR part to receive them. We must remember that healing is part of our covenant with God, but that **in every covenant, BOTH sides must be committed to fulfilling their responsibility.** When we begin to study the promises of God in His Word, we find that there are **conditions** involved with receiving every promise! We are quick to claim the promises of God, but we must also be careful to consider the **whole counsel of God concerning a subject.**

Several years ago, God made this very clear to me when I was asked to speak at a Sunday morning service at an inner city night shelter, where most of the participants were homeless. The minister who asked me said he felt God's direction to have me speak. I began to pray about it intensely, because I couldn't imagine what God could have me say to a group of homeless people!! Immediately the Holy Spirit responded by telling me, "I want you to ask them if they've ever had a dream for their life, and if they realize that their dream came from Me! I want you to tell them that the circumstances they're in right now have never been MY plan for them and that for the most part, their own CHOICES are what put them where they are, but that I have a better plan!"

He told me to tell them that He loved them, and that what He really wanted from them was a **relationship.** He directed me to John 15:7, which says: "If you live in Me [**abide vitally united to Me**] and My words remain in you and continue to live in your hearts, ask whatever you will, and it shall be done for you." (Amplified, my emphasis) God showed me clearly that two of the most important words in this passage are "IF" and "ABIDE." "Abiding" with Him means living and walking with Him DAILY, **vitally united to Him in relationship. If** we are truly abiding with Him, we will hunger and thirst after His Word, which will live IN us, and **in that case**, God will be willing to answer any prayer we pray.

He then gave me this example from everyday life to which the people at the shelter could relate. He said to tell them this: "Imagine you're a father with two sons. One of your sons loves you so much that he never wants to be away from you. When you get up in the morning, he wants to have breakfast with you, and he loves going places with you. On the days that you work, he wants to go to work with you and go fishing with you when you get home. He loves to discuss things with you and ask your advice, and when he goes to bed at night, he wants you to tuck him in and love on him. He tells you regularly that he loves you."

"Your other son can always find something better to do than to spend time with you. His friends, past-times, and activities always seem more important to him than his relationship with you. He doesn't ever seek your advice or your consolation, and he doesn't really show an interest in your work or in anything else that you do. He's never around, because he's too busy with the things HE wants to do. Tell me, when it comes time for you to make a trip to the ice cream store, which son do you think will get an ice cream first?" This, of course, was an analogy to OUR relationship with God the Father. If we're praying persistently in faith for something, and believe God will give it to us but we're not seeing the answer, maybe we need to consider **relationship**! ("**If** you live in Me and My words remain in you, **ask whatever you will.....**") (My emphasis)

There is no Scripture that says or implies that God prefers our physical well-being over that of our spirit or soul—in fact, a number of Scriptures indicate that His priority for us is for the peace of our spirit and soul! One such Scripture is found in Romans 8: 6, which says: "For to be **carnally minded is death,** but to be spiritually minded is **life and peace**." (My emphasis) As our Heavenly Father, God knows us so well that He knows about the person who will seek God for physical healing, and after he receives it, God won't hear from that person again until he "needs" something else from God. God MAY NOT grant physical healing for a period of time because **there is something more important that He needs to do in the realm of the soul.** The Holy Spirit spoke so clearly and gave me this example to explain that God's role as our Heavenly "Father" encompasses some of what human fathers feel:

He said, "IF you had a choice here on Earth of having a

child who was completely well physically but did not know God, OR having a child with some physical affliction who was walking with God, seeking and living God's will for his life, submitted to God and therefore receiving God's blessings of peace of mind, joy, happiness, contentment and fulfillment that comes about as a RESULT of that relationship with God, which would you choose for your child?" **Jesus also died so that we might have our peace** ("the chastisement for our peace was upon Him," Is. 53: 5), **and the joy of living a committed and submitted life**! God wants it ALL for us, but He also has a PLAN to bring us to **complete victory** in our individual lives!

He went on to say: "That's why sometimes people must wait for the manifestation of their physical healing, because God knows that without the 'harvest of peace and righteousness' (referred to in Hebrews 12:11) that is produced while they're waiting on the Lord and **submitted to the discipline of His Word**—without this harvest—the physical healing will still leave those people with an 'emptiness' in their soul, lacking ALL that God has for them." **God knows that for many of us, if we received healing the first time we asked God for it, we would never have to persevere in prayer, in the Word, in our relationship with Him, or in faith, and we would also never mature in those areas.**

Another example in the natural to parallel God's "fatherly love" is that some parents give their children material **(physical) things** to try to compensate for the lack of time, love and attention they give them. We have all seen examples of children who grow up in this type of home environment, and we know that in almost every case, these **children who are devoid of love and time spent with their parents become emotionally damaged in some way. As our loving "Heavenly Father," God doesn't want His children to turn out this way**....His greatest desire is to spend time with us and to show us His love. We always want the **physical healing** and God wants it for us, but He also recognizes that **abiding** with Him and in His Word is vital to completing the picture of our wholeness!

God's plan for man was that we be in total fellowship and communication with Him—that's what He wants more than anything! He wants us to be so in touch with Him that we KNOW His plan for us, because He loves us so much and knows that HIS plan for us is the best possible! **Our relationship with God is much more important to Him than what we DO for Him,** because if the relationship isn't there, then what we DO for Him is either "dead works" or a show of "religious practice"! **When we truly ABIDE with Him daily, which means walking, talking, and fellowshipping with Him, and when His Word lives IN us, then we'll want to do the things that please Him, because we've experienced His love first-hand and know that He really IS our "Heavenly Father"!**

When we're abiding with Him daily, we'll learn to hear His voice and to know Him better. His plan for us will become the desire of OUR hearts! Wholeness in the realm of the soul begins when we learn to abide with Him, because it is only THEN that our mind, our will, and our emotions start to conform to HIS WILL. **When we get to the point where we can honestly say that we desire the will and plan of God for our life more than we desire anything else, we can be sure that we have truly matured in our walk with God—we are THEN closer to becoming "whole" than we've ever been!**

Sometimes the problem in our prayers is that we are actually asking God for the wrong thing! **Many times people pray for physical healing, when what God wants them to see is that there is something in the realm of the soul that is the true "root" cause of the sickness.** Even medical doctors who aren't Christians now realize that damaged emotions and stress are the real cause of many physical illnesses. God knows that He may heal the physical part, but that illness may come back if the problem in the realm of the soul (the mind, will or emotions) is not healed as well.

Our Lord is very capable and wants to heal **every part of us**, but He wants us to recognize and acknowledge the source of the problem! He said to ASK for wisdom concerning this, and it will be given to you! James 1: 2 and 4-6 gives us a wonderful explanation of how our seeking God for wisdom concerning "trials of any sort" or "temptations" can ultimately bring us in to **wholeness:** "Consider it wholly joyful, my brethren, whenever you are enveloped in or encounter **trials of any sort or fall into various temptations....**But let endurance and steadfastness and patience have full play and do a thorough work, **so that you may be [people] perfectly and fully developed [with no defects], lacking in nothing. If any of you is deficient in wisdom, let him ask of the giving God [Who gives] to everyone** liberally and ungrudgingly, without reproaching or fault-finding, **and it will be given him. Only it must be in faith that he asks with no wavering (no hesitating, no doubting)....**" (Amplified, my emphasis)

How can we receive healing for something we can't or won't even acknowledge, and how could God receive the glory for it?? When it's revealed to us, we can then pray and use the resources God has provided to keep us strong and to realize that we have had the victory! We need to be asking for a "**spirit of wisdom and revelation**" as also suggested in Ephesians Chapter One, so that we know where our true weakness lies. Satan is constantly seeking those whom he may destroy by reminding them of their past life and former temptations! He also tries hard to make people believe they weren't REALLY healed after all!

If someone has been praying and believing God for physical healing but hasn't received the manifestation, **in**

some cases it may be because he has willfully disobeyed God, or is deliberately sinning. Unconfessed sin can be a definite hindrance to receiving healing. I Corinthians 11:27-30 warns us that even taking communion in an unworthy manner can cause sickness or death! **Not all sickness is caused by sin, however**, as Jesus pointed out in John 9:3 when He was asked who sinned to cause the man's blindness from birth: "It was not that this man or his parents sinned, but **he was born blind in order that the workings of God should be manifested (displayed and illustrated) in him.**" (Amplified, my emphasis)

Here Jesus is clearly telling those who ask that this man's blindness and subsequent healing **was for God's glory**—to display His goodness and mercy! **But God cannot be glorified if WE do not seek His healing, expect it, and wait for His timing and plan to receive it!**

In John Chapter 5, Jesus mercifully healed the lame man at the pool of Bethesda, but in verse 14, He also **warned the man: "See, you are well! Stop sinning or something worse may happen to you**." (Amplified, my emphasis) Our sinning gives Satan an "opening" to come in and inflict physical, mental, or emotional harm upon us. **When a person engages in sin time after time** and does not seek the help of the Holy Spirit and the authority of the Blood to help him stop sinning, **his separation from God will eventually and inevitably bring about physical, mental or emotional crisis, because his spirit will be "at war" with his body and soul. Sooner or later, a spiritual crisis will always affect some other realm of a person's being.**

In further considering the counsel of the Word of God concerning answered prayer, we find that James 5:16 tells us: "**Confess your trespasses** to one another, and pray for one another **that you may be healed**. The effective, fervent prayer of a righteous man **avails much**." (My emphasis) The implication here is that our prayers will "carry more weight" with God if we are in right standing with Him and have confessed our sin before we ask Him for something! We are today seeing miracles of God's grace, however, toward people who are not even Christians, because God knows that a physical miracle will bring **those people** to Him! Romans 2:4 says that "….God's kindness is intended to lead you to repent (to change your mind and inner man to accept God's will)…." (Amplified)

The Bible presents stories of different conditions and diversities of healings for a reason—to show us that God will touch us in the way that WE need to be touched as an individual in order for His purposes to come about in our lives. In my own case, I have been praying for and believing God for healing for many, many years. I've had no reason to doubt that God heals miraculously, because He touched me and healed me of a terrible migraine in the privacy of my own room when I was 21 years old. I had been calling out to God, and then I heard the voice of the Holy Spirit say "Linda….Because of your FAITH, you will be blessed!" The glory of God came on me, and I felt like I was "frozen" to the bed! Suddenly a sensation like electricity went from my head down into my toes, and the migraine and sickness were instantly gone!

Because of this experience, my faith in God's healing power is strong, and I know that if God cared enough to heal me of a headache, He cares that I suffer every day. I have no doubt that my healing is already "done," even though I haven't SEEN it yet in the flesh. **I have never given up on God's promise of healing, and I will remain steadfast until I see the manifestation of it in my body!!** However, it has become very clear to me that there is no one "formula" for healing that works for everyone. I believe that God heals in HIS time, in HIS way, for HIS purposes in our lives! Ecclesiastes Chapter 3 says there is "a time for everything," and verse 3 states, "a time to kill and **a time to heal**."

(My emphasis) It's not a question of whether God **wants** you to be healed; it's a question of TIMING and God's ORDER for your life!

Several years ago, God began speaking to me through Scriptures, prophesies and in other ways that my own healing was going to be manifested when I stepped into my office of healing ministry. He showed me that it goes along with the Biblical principle that you will "reap what you sow" into others' lives, and one of the Scriptures He gave me as confirmation was Isaiah 58: 6-11. This has since then been confirmed to me over and over again, by prophetic word given to me, and by the voice of the Holy Spirit spoken to me in times of prayer. Many Christians will vehemently deny that God "works that way"....but, if He gives you a specific word pertaining to your situation, then that is the way He will work to bring about results in **your** life.

In praying about this one day and asking God to help me understand what He was telling me, He reminded me of the story of the woman with the issue of blood, who received her healing after many years when she **took a step of faith** and touched the hem of Jesus' garment. The Holy Spirit spoke to me that "The reason many of you receive your own healing when you step into the office of healing ministry is because that IS your step of faith!! And it's a much GREATER step of faith than most people take, because you're not only believing for your own healing, you're believing for the healing of many others that you will minister to under my power!" It is also a matter of walking in **obedience and surrender** to what you know God has called you to do. There are many examples in Scripture of blessings coming to those walking in obedience to God, and curses coming to those who disobey. Deuteronomy Chapter 28 is one passage that spells them out for us!

Luke Chapter 17 tells us the story of the ten lepers who called to Jesus from a distance to have pity on them. The only thing Jesus said to them was for them to go and show themselves to the priests, and **as they went**, they were healed. This story is an example of Jesus' response to **obedience**. The ten lepers did not question Jesus, **they simply did what He said to do and received their healing as a result**! By obeying Jesus, they also showed that they had faith that Jesus would heal them, because the law required going to a priest **after** you were cured of a disease.

Then there is the case of the person who may not receive the manifestation of his healing because he is expecting God to do something for him that he should be doing for himself! I truly believe that in most cases, God is not going to do something for you that you can do for yourself! If the answer to our physical problem can be found in a change of our diet or exercise, or even in keeping a healthy attitude, God expects us to do what we can to help ourselves!! He expects us to be good caretakers of the "temple" in which He resides—our body!

It seems to me that the proof that many people are beginning to realize this is the great resurgence of interest in nutrition and natural medicine that has taken place in the past couple of decades. Many are discovering that there are natural remedies—foods, vitamins, and herbs—that they can use **to help themselves bring about healing in their bodies**, without risking the effects of chemical drugs. Over the centuries, people in every culture have recognized that God created herbs, plants, fruits and vegetables for the health of the human body! We simply cannot eat a steady diet of unhealthy foods and expect to have a healthy body! Many have also begun to realize the importance of physical exercise to the health of the body.

One way that we can ALL help ourselves is to MAKE ourselves be cheerful, rejoice, praise, and yes, laugh—even when our "flesh" doesn't FEEL like doing it!! Proverbs 17:22 says that "A happy heart is good medicine and **a**

cheerful mind works healing, but a broken spirit dries up the bones." (Amplified, my emphasis) The bones contain marrow, which is where red blood cells are produced. We know that without full, rich marrow in our bones, we will not be healthy! A broken spirit always drains our strength! **Many things that are being discovered in various fields of science are actually confirming "scientifically" what God has already said in His Word!**

An interesting series of studies done at Loma Linda University in California was recently published by a "laugh researcher" named Lee Berk. Berk measured the effects of laughter on the immune system by checking blood markers every ten minutes. He divided subjects into two groups and hooked them up to IV's. Half were shown a video of a comedian, and the other half sat quietly in a room. The blood samples were taken every ten minutes during the video and thirty minutes afterward.

The control group showed no change; however, the video watchers had significant increases in various immune function measures in the blood. The increases were documented in activated T cells, which battle infection; natural killer cells, which attack tumors and microbes; immunoglobulin A antibodies, which safeguard the respiratory tract; and gamma interferon, a major immune system messenger. Cortisol is a hormone that suppresses the immune system; their levels of this hormone were significantly lower after the laughing session!

Berk is convinced that laughter is a state of "eustress," which means the opposite of distress. He says stressful emotions such as grief and anger can suppress the immune system, while positive emotions, such as mirth, can strengthen it. To put it in other words, laughter creates its own "physiological state," says Berk, with changes in the immune system which are the opposite to those caused by stress.(2) Something as simple as laughter is a positive way that any of us could help our own health much more than we could have ever imagined! **The Bible's assertion that "A happy heart is good medicine" can be verified as scientific truth through the study of the natural blood!**

Although God is performing many miracles of healing today, we must not forget that **sometimes healing comes in other ways besides miracles.** There are many doctors, nutritionists, chiropractors and other practitioners who are truly called by God to do what they do—and often God will direct us to one of them to **help bring about** our healing. Ultimately, however, all healing comes from God, because He IS "Jehovah-Rapha," our Healer! Beware of any practitioner who refers to **himself** as the "healer" and doesn't give God the glory for your healing!

In John 9:6-7, we see an example of the healing of a blind man's eyes: "….He spat on the ground and made clay [mud] with His saliva, and He spread it [as ointment] on the man's eyes. And He said to him, Go, wash in the Pool of Siloam—which means Sent. So he went and washed, and came back seeing." (Amplified) In this instance, we see that a natural substance was used as a means of healing. Jesus told the man to "Go" and then told him what else to do—to wash in the pool. This shows us that God may ordain that healing take place through a natural substance or even a pharmaceutical medicine, and that at times, there may be other instructions (from a practitioner or from God Himself) that we need to follow to receive our healing.

In talking or preaching about God's desire to heal everyone, some will say that "Jesus never refused to heal anyone," as an argument for the fact that one should expect healing immediately when prayed for. It is true that Jesus never refused anyone, according to the Scriptures. However, as we've already seen, there are examples of healing in the New Testament that indicate that, for some people, there was a **process** to their healing, or an element of submission and obedience that was necessary to receive it. **Healing in the New Testament was not always "instant"!**

An obvious example of this is found in Mark 8:22-25, where another blind man was brought to Jesus. Verse 23 says, "....And when He had spit on his eyes and put His hands on him, **He asked him if he saw anything**. And he looked up and said, 'I see men like trees, walking.' **Then he put his hands on his eyes again** and made him look up. **And he was restored and saw everyone clearly**." (My emphasis) Jesus wouldn't have asked the man **"if he saw anything" if He hadn't realized that there would be a process to this man's healing!** This is clearly showing that healing for some people will take place gradually, through a process that God chooses. This fact should bring comfort and reassurance to those who don't receive their complete healing "instantly" when prayed for....They only need to keep **standing in faith** and trusting God to see the "process" completed!

Often we hear Christians telling people that they haven't received their healing because they "don't have enough faith." While this may be true for some people, I know that in my own case, a lack of faith has nothing to do with waiting for my healing. Jesus told the disciples in Matthew 17:20 that if they only had faith the size of a mustard seed, which is very tiny, they could command mountains to move! I know that I personally have MUCH GREATER faith than that, and that many other Christians who pray for healing do also! Telling someone that all they need is just "more faith" can be very harmful and misleading, because some Christians KNOW they have plenty of faith and they become very frustrated trying to figure out how to get more! They are led to believe that that's ALL they need to receive their healing.

I have also heard several ministers over the years tell people to "Place a **demand** on the anointing"! This gives the impression that **we** are in charge, not God! The anointing is the presence and power of God that comes to effect change in peoples' lives. When someone says to place a demand on the "anointing," they are really saying "demand it of God." Nowhere in the Bible does it say that we as humans can demand **anything** of God! We can, and should, **ask**....we can, and should, **expect**....we can, and should, **believe....but we don't receive anything from God by demanding it!**

Healing comes because, out of God's love, mercy, sovereignty and omniscience, He grants it to an individual that **He** has determined is ready to receive it! But we must understand that His thoughts and His ways are not the same as ours. He does as He pleases, in His way, in His perfect timing! Your healing will come about **in the way and in the time that He has ordained it for you**. One of my favorite Bible verses is **Psalm 138:8: "The Lord will perfect that which concerns me**.**"** (My emphasis) How awesome! THAT's how much He cares about us!!

What some people really need is a change in their prayer life—to get down to the "basics" with God and start asking questions such as: "Is there anything **in me** that is keeping me from receiving my healing—disobedience or sin?" "Is there anything I should be doing myself to help bring about my own healing?" "What is the ROOT of my illness?" "Am I holding on to harmful emotions such as bitterness, uncontrolled anger, resentment, unforgiveness, jealousy or hatred?" "Am I seeking and submitting to Your will for my life?" "What is Your plan for my healing?" We need to fervently and sincerely seek His answers, then be attuned to the voice and the direction of the Holy Spirit in our lives.

It's not likely that God will respond to continuous "begging" for healing, or for anything else, for that matter, because begging implies a lack of trust and peace concerning God's will for our wholeness. This is not to say that

persistence in prayer is wrong, however—it is actually very Biblical! What really pleases Him, and what He responds to, besides faith, is a humble heart, someone who is seeking His face and who truly has right motivations in wanting to please Him. We need to be asking for the right thing!

As Christians, we should always pray believing that our healing is already accomplished through the shed Blood of Jesus. But if we've been in dozens of healing services and many prayer lines, and we've been praying for our own healing for months or years and still have not seen the manifestation of it, we need to ask God for wisdom in discerning WHY. Remember that whatever God is doing in your life, He is doing for the ultimate purpose of seeing you become a WHOLE person. His timing is perfect for **your needs**!

God's plan was that the health of the physical, spiritual, mental and emotional aspects of our being would each be intricately dependent upon the health of the other three! Just as the blood in our natural bodies is created with antibodies, nutrients, enzymes and hormones to provide what is needed to keep you alive, the Blood atonement of Jesus assures us that God works in our lives in every way He can to keep us "alive" physically, spiritually, mentally and emotionally. "We are assured and know that [God being a partner in their labor] **all things work together and are [fitting into a plan] for good** to and for those who love God and are called according to [His] design and purpose."(Rom.8:28, Amplified, my emphasis) Thank God that His ultimate plan for us is for complete **wholeness** in every area of our lives!

CHAPTER 6

Maintaining Our "Spiritual pH"

Interestingly enough, the Holy Spirit has revealed some other aspects of spiritual maturity through another avenue of study in the natural—the subject of pH. In working in the field of natural medicine, I came to realize the vital importance of such a seemingly insignificant thing as pH in the human body. I say "seemingly insignificant" because it is a subject that allopathic, or traditional, doctors very rarely address or even mention to their patients, and therefore, **most people never think of it in connection with a disease process.**

The fact is, however, that pH is present in every living thing on the earth, including the soil! That in itself would seem to indicate its importance. **Maintaining proper pH levels is vital to sustaining life!** Normal pH levels are important for body functioning because even small changes in pH can produce major changes in metabolism. It is essential that blood pH levels remain in an extremely narrow range—between 7.35 and 7.45 is considered "normal" range. If blood pH falls to 7.0, the same as water, a person will probably go into an acidotic coma that may be fatal. If the blood pH rises above 7.5, a person would lapse into a condition called "tetany," which is marked by severe muscle spasms, and the person would probably die. So an extremely acid or alkaline blood pH can be fatal! Every fluid in our bodies must maintain a "normal" pH, or the body will do whatever it needs to do to compensate for the abnormality—with "unhealthy results"!(1)

The term "pH" stands for "potential of Hydrogen," and is a measurement of the relative acidity or alkalinity of a solution, but can also be seen as a measure of the ENERGY you're able to produce from the food you've taken in. In other words, it is an indicator of how your body is using nutrients, and what kind of "ash" the foods you're eating are leaving—acid ash or alkaline ash. If you're like most Americans, the majority of your daily diet (75-95%) consists of acid ash-producing foods, which are the cause of a lot of trouble, if consumed excessively. Some of the main culprits in this category are dairy products, animal protein, refined foods, and "junk" food.(2)

Our bodies have an alkaline reserve, made up of minerals that help compensate for the bad effects of dietary acid ash. The body uses organic minerals to buffer or neutralize dietary acid ash, the most important of which is sodium, but it can also use calcium, potassium, and magnesium. The main source of these organic minerals is fruits and vegetables—the foods God has provided in nature. Because God created us, He knew that these foods He also created would provide essential minerals to keep our bodies in balance. We tamper with God's perfect "order" for our bodies and reap the results when we give in to eating man's fabricated foods over God's perfectly created ones.(3)

The acid-producing foods leave strong acids that are hard for our bodies to get rid of, but all of our cells also produce a weak acid that is easily eliminated through the lungs. The only cells that **don't have the capability of producing acids are MATURE red blood cells!**(4) Remember this as we follow some analogies!

In our natural bodies, everything we eat AFFECTS our pH and is AFFECTED BY our pH. Merriam-Webster's Online Dictionary defines "acid" as: "(1a): Sour, sharp, or biting to the taste; (1b): Sharp, biting, or sour in manner, disposition or nature."....(5) In comparing to the spiritual realm, if we don't get enough of the right kind of "**spiritual food**," (the Word of God), or if it's not properly "utilized"....we are very likely to become "too acid"— sharp, biting or sour in our manner toward other people AND in our attitude toward God when things go wrong!!

On the other hand, a bitter or sharply critical attitude toward others will also have an effect on **how we receive the Word of God**—our "flesh" may very well resist the correction and conviction that the Word is intended to bring! This can be seen as a warning to us concerning something that can **prevent** our maturing in Christ and keep us from achieving wholeness in the Body of Christ. **As we MATURE in Christ, our dispositions and attitudes toward others should become less and less "acid"!! When we as Christians allow our attitudes and dispositions toward others to remain too "acid"—(sharp, biting, and bitter)—a "disease" process begins and can spread throughout the Body of Christ....a very "unhealthy" condition** which leads to division and disorder in the Body. (This spiritual "disease" process, if allowed to continue in the individual, can also eventually result in actual physical or mental disease in that individual. The Bible warns against negative emotions because they endanger our "wholeness" in so many ways!)

That is why Jesus said in John 15:7 that the Word must "**abide in us**"! How many times do we see the bitter, negative reactions and attitudes of Christians in the church against their brothers and sisters for the slightest provocation—the very people that we are to love, encourage, nurture, and build up in the faith? And how many so-called Christians in history have turned their backs on God and become bitter toward Him because of a tragedy in their lives….the One who is the very **source** of our life and blessings! How quickly we can forget who our Source IS!! It reminds me of the sign I saw on the front lawn of a church that read: "Why is it that we call Him 'Our Father' on Sunday and act like orphans the rest of the week?"

We can tell in the human body about the energy being produced by our food by taking readings of a person's urine and saliva pH. But we can also tell how well a person is "absorbing" and making use of **spiritual food** by observing **the energy of their faith.** Is it generating "life" to others? Is it reflecting the **power** and the glory of God?

We must let the Word renew our heart, mind, and spirit so that we can do what it says in Revelation 12:11—overcome him (Satan) by the Blood of the Lamb and the word of our testimony! Our testimony IS the Word—we have to first have it **abiding in us** so that we know it, and then **use it** together with the Blood to overcome! Are you using the Word as your spiritual nourishment and then applying the Blood to produce spiritual "energy"? (That's the POWER!)

Just as our "acid ash-producing" diet can adversely affect our health and even cause death in extreme cases, the unhealthy things that we "feed" our mind, emotions, and spirit with can not only make us sick in mind, body, and spirit, but a steady "diet" of worldly things can quench the Holy Spirit in us and bring us "spiritual death." Consider the ill effects of provocative, sexually explicit and violent movies, television programming, video games, music and printed materials that have invaded our society and our minds. We should not be surprised that as we have allowed these influences in our society to become more pervasive, our crime rates have soared, as well as the incidence of mental illness and chronic physical sickness.

The United States has the greatest educational system and most advanced medical technologies in the world, yet according to a Justice Department study, one in every 150 Americans was incarcerated in a jail or prison in mid-1998, a rate of incarceration double that of twelve years before. We also have great numbers of chronically ill people in our population, and heart disease is the number one killer in our country. It is not really surprising that "heart" disease is the number one killer, because the Bible says in Proverbs 4:23 to "Keep and **guard your heart** with all vigilance and **above all that you guard, for out of it flow the springs of life**"! (Amplified, my emphasis) Our very life in the flesh is dependent upon how much influence the Word of God and the Cross of Christ have on us!! When will we realize that, the more we let the perverse things of the world influence our thoughts, emotions and spirits, the more Satan will gain a foothold on us as he seeks to "kill, steal, and destroy"! Satan definitely knows where our weaknesses lie, and he takes every opportunity to "capitalize" on them!

I Thessalonians 5:23 says: "Now may the God of peace Himself **sanctify you** completely; and **may your whole spirit, soul and body be preserved blameless** at the coming of our Lord Jesus Christ." (My emphasis) One of the main ways we can accomplish this is to make every effort to avoid the temptations and snares of the world's forms of "entertainment"! Another evidence of the seriousness of Satan's efforts against Christians is in the shocking numbers of Christian men and even pastors who have fallen victim to the temptation of internet pornography. Its easy access and insidious nature have been instrumental in the breakup of too many families and marriages in recent years.

The stronghold that this addiction carries has been too much for even pastors to overcome, and sadly for some of them, their families and ministries have fallen apart as a result. If only they would realize that the Blood of Jesus can help give them overcoming power to **defend their minds** against anything! Remember that "....God is faithful, who will not allow you to be tempted beyond what you are able, **but with the temptation will also make the way of escape, that you may be able to bear it.**" (I Cor. 10:13, my emphasis)

I have personally discovered this ability of the Blood of Jesus to "defend the mind," as over the years I have become frustrated during my prayer times in letting my mind "wander" and my own thoughts enter in as I "wait" on the Holy Spirit. I have discovered that, when I come to the point during my prayer time that I need to hear from the Holy Spirit, I first "plead the Blood of Jesus over my mind and my thoughts, that no other thoughts except those of the Holy Spirit may enter in." I then ask for God to let me hear from Him "unstained" as I sit and wait on the Holy Spirit. I always have an assurance and a peace that, when I do this, what I "hear" will be from the Holy Spirit, and not my own thoughts, or thoughts that the enemy might put in my head.

Again we can observe a parallel between the natural and spiritual in a diagram which I often used in my practice that shows a simplistic view of how a molecule of pH is formed. Two types of ions, anabolic or "an-ions" and catabolic or "cat-ions" come together to form a molecule of pH. Cat-ions are acid, and come from our food, and an-ions are alkaline and are formed mostly in the liver. So cat-ions come from an external source, and an-ions from an internal source. Here's how it looks:

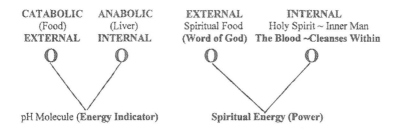

CATABOLIC	ANABOLIC	EXTERNAL	INTERNAL
(Food)	(Liver)	Spiritual Food	Holy Spirit ~ Inner Man
EXTERNAL	INTERNAL	(Word of God)	The Blood ~Cleanses Within
O	O	O	O

pH Molecule (Energy Indicator)   Spiritual Energy (Power)

In the spiritual, the Word of God, (which is "**external**") together with the Blood's cleansing power from **within** and the Holy Spirit's revelation and **inner witness**, produce an "**immeasurable and unlimited and surpassing greatness of His power in and for us** who believe, as demonstrated in the working of His mighty strength, **which He exerted in Christ when He raised Him from the dead** and seated Him at His [own] right hand in the heavenly [places]...." (Ephesians 1:19-20, Amplified, my emphasis) **That power is what we call the "anointing"!** It is truly awesome to think that we have IN us the same power that raised Christ from the dead! What power in the universe could be more impressive than that? It is what enables us to minister effectively to others, and to stay strong and "at peace" when everything around us is falling apart! It is what enables us to have joy even when our circumstances don't look "joyful"!

"Catabolism" is defined by Merriam-Webster's Online Dictionary as coming from a Greek word, *katabolE*, which means "throwing down." It is "destructive metabolism involving the release of **energy** and resulting in the **breakdown** of complex materials within the organism."(6) It involves a process of **"breaking down,"** as food must be first broken down in order to be used in the body. In its parallel with "the Word," which must be "taken in," we see in Hebrews 4:12 (Amplified, my emphasis) that: "....the Word that God speaks is alive and full of power [making it active, operative, **energizing**, and effective]; it is sharper than any two-edged sword, **penetrating** to the dividing line of the breath of life (soul) and [the immortal] spirit, and of joints and marrow [of the deepest parts of our nature], exposing and sifting and **analyzing and judging** the very thoughts and purposes of the heart." **When we analyze something, we "break it down"!! The Word of God also has the power to** "break down" walls and strongholds and bring conviction to our hearts when we hear it spoken! Furthermore, it will **penetrate** the hearts of men and reveal **truth** to us— the Word is our standard against which the truth of anything should be **judged**!

"Anabolism," on the other hand, is defined as "The **constructive** part of metabolism concerned especially with macromolecular synthesis," (7) or, to put it in other terms, it is a process of **"building up."** The fruit of the Holy Spirit within us "....is love, joy, peace, longsuffering, kindness, goodness, faithfulness, gentleness, self-control." (Gal. 5:22) These fruits obviously **build us up** as individuals and ulti-mately **build up the Church**. Romans 8:26 says; "Likewise the Spirit also **helps in our weaknesses**. For we do not know what we should pray for as we ought, but the Spirit Himself makes intercession for us with groanings which cannot be uttered." (My emphasis) And in Acts 1:8, Jesus spoke these words to the apostles: "But you shall receive **power** when the Holy Spirit has come upon you...." In so many other ways, **the Holy Spirit "builds us up":** as our Counselor, Encourager, Teacher, Comforter, and Exhorter!!

As a final analogy, **the precious Blood of Jesus "builds us up"** from within as it cleanses us, protects us, and gives us **power** to minister and to resist Satan! Jesus left us well "equipped" when he left us here on Earth! We have the prescription to live a life of wholeness, minister to others with power from above, and to be strengthened and encour-aged by the living Word of God! We have all the equipment we need to live a life of victory!! **I believe that if many Christians will begin to meditate upon and claim the power of the Blood of Jesus in their lives, they will SEE that victory first-hand, in every area of their lives!**

When we honestly examine and reflect upon the amazing parallels between the spiritual and the natural, it is hard to deny that the universe exudes a plan of "intelligent design" which can only be attributed to a mighty and supernatural Power! The evidence is all around us—and is still being revealed—that the design in nature and the human body are no "quirk of fate" or "accidental" happening—there has always been a Plan, orchestrated by the Master Designer!!

CHAPTER 7

The "Salt of the Earth"

M ost of us think of salt mainly as a seasoning for food, although it has been estimated that there are more than 14,000 uses for it! **Various salts together with water are actually the mineral constituents of the human body, and are essential to the functioning of the body's cells**. About 0.9 per cent of the blood and body cells consist of salt. Our blood, sweat and tears are all salty.(1)

There are more than thirty references to salt in the Bible, in both the Old and New Testament. In ancient times, salt was considered a **preservative** and a **precious commodity**, and was also regarded as a symbol of **purity and permanence** in the Bible.(2) In Leviticus 2:13, the Israelites were instructed to add salt to all of their offerings, to signify the preservation of their covenant with God, and the permanence of it. Jesus tells the disciples in Matthew 5:13, "You are the salt of the earth...." **A little deeper study will show us some of the reasons that salt was implicated with spiritual matters in God's Word, and why Jesus saw His disciples as the "salt of the earth."**

Some of the general functions that salts perform in the

human body are:

1) Salts maintain **water balance and blood volume**.(3) As we saw in Chapter One, the Blood of Jesus and the "Living Water," the Holy Spirit, are essential to our maintaining **spiritual balance.** When we are fulfilling our role as the "salt" of the earth, we will communicate to others two of the vital sources of "balance" in the Christian's walk with God: **the Blood and the Living Water**! We have already seen that they are inseparably linked!

As we witness, we need to be imparting to the new believer an understanding of the Blood Covenant. Without this understanding, one will never truly grasp the relationship between the Old and the New Testament, nor will he understand what "belongs" to him as a child of God and an heir of the Blood Covenant. The deposit of the "Living Water" into the spirit of a new believer brings about the transformation necessary to help that person become the "salt" to the world, as the love of God begins to grow in his heart. The Holy Spirit in him also gives the revelation to understand the Word of God, which is another essential element in our "balance." The Word of God must be "living" in our hearts, just as the water and blood in our bodies keeps us living.

2) Salt maintains proper **acid-base balance**.(4) In other words, it is a compound that results when a base neutralizes an acid.(5) As the "salt of the earth," our attitudes and relationships with others should be such that we help to "neutralize" the effects of the sharp, biting or sour dispositions and talk that people so easily fall into—**(the problem of maintaining our "spiritual pH").** Instead of encouraging these negative things in our human nature, we can and should be helping to **neutralize** them by not entering into conversations and behaviors that perpetuate the "acid" or bitter viewpoint in ourselves or in others! As the salt, we should help to offset bitterness in the emotional realm with

the truth of the healing Blood flow of Jesus that takes care of our whole being! Jesus died to set the captive free from crippling emotions!

3) Salt maintains the proper conditions for **coagulation, or clotting of the blood.**(6) By ministering and witnessing to others as the "salt," we can be instruments to bring them to the saving knowledge of Christ. This affords them the benefits of the **protective seal of the New Blood Covenant**, and **binds them together** with the Body of Christ, the Church. That "protective seal" positions them for victory over the wounds the enemy tries to inflict, as well as giving the victory in the struggle with our own flesh!

4) Salt regulates **cell membrane and capillary permeability.**(7) This refers to the condition of the capillary walls that allows substances in the blood to **spread** into tissues or cells. As the "salt" of the earth, we are called upon to **spread the news** of what the Blood of Jesus has done, so that the reality of it **permeates hearts and minds. Our speech, our attitudes, and our lives must exemplify to others that the Blood of Jesus made us truly free** from the bondages of sin, sickness, depression, guilt, harmful emotions, and poverty! If we don't show it, where is the power in our testimony? What is the FRUIT of our witness?

In Mark 9:50, Jesus also tells the disciples, "Have salt within yourselves, and be at peace and live in harmony with one another." (Amplified) Jesus here is encouraging the disciples (and US) **to let our purifying influence permeate** the Body of Christ and the world, just as salt permeates our bodies. **Salt symbolized purity in ancient times**, and we as disciples are to also be an example to the world of the purity and holiness of God.

Salt has throughout history been used as a **preservative. As the "salt of the earth," we represent the preservation of the Blood Covenant passed down from Abraham to all generations**. As salt in the natural "cures" things and makes them better to eat over time, so our New Blood Covenant has better promises than the original! Our lives should also **preserve** the image of Christ in the world! The image of Christ-likeness that we display should be **preserved** in us more and more over time, as we grow up into maturity in Christ.

II Corinthians 3:17-18 expounds upon this process: "Now the Lord is the Spirit, and where the Spirit of the Lord is, there is liberty (emancipation from bondage, freedom). And all of us, as with unveiled face, [because we] continued to behold [in the Word of God] as in a mirror the glory of the Lord, **are constantly being transfigured into His very own image in ever increasing splendor and from one degree of glory to another; [for this comes] from the Lord [Who is] the Spirit.**" (Amplified, my emphasis)

Salt also **enhances** the flavor of food. Colossians 4:6 admonishes us to "Let your speech always be with grace, **seasoned with salt**, that you may know how you ought to answer each one."(My emphasis) Our spiritual food, the Word of God, should flow out of us and reflect the grace and love of God in our lives, in order to **enhance the lives of others**. Ephesians 4:29 says, "Let no foul or polluting language, nor evil word, nor unwholesome or worthless talk [ever] come out of your mouth, but only such [speech] **as is good and beneficial to the spiritual progress of others,** as is fitting to the need and the occasion, **that it may be a blessing and give grace (God's favor) to those who hear it.**" (Amplified, my emphasis) What we speak to others should be appealing enough to give them an **appetite** for the things of God!

Another parallel we can see is in the "sacrifices" of blood, sweat and tears that Jesus shed on the cross. According to Leviticus 2:13, every grain offering that was brought to the altar was to be **salted**, as a memorial to the permanence of the covenant God had made with the

Israelites. In the new and better covenant that has been passed down to us, **the sacrifices that Jesus made of blood, sweat and tears permeated with salt** are a reminder to us that as the "salt of the earth," **we are to be "salty living sacrifices"**! We need to be always willing to sacrifice our time, money, comfort, or whatever else we are required to in order to fulfill the destiny God has for us, and to be obedient to Him. As God's people with a mandate to "go into all the world," our "salt shakers" should always remain FULL!!

Through my experience with the practice God called me to, I came to realize that **God wants to make a covenant with each one of us**, which is the destiny for our individual lives. In order to seal the covenant, the first step is that we must be in such a relationship with Him that we make it our heart's desire to **seek His face and hear His voice** so that we KNOW THAT WE KNOW what His plan IS for our life! The next step is to seek His constant direction in all that we do, so that His plan can be fulfilled **through our willingness**! Then we must walk in obedience and submission to His plan, as we feed on His Word and fortify our determination that NOTHING will keep us from fulfilling it! Whatever God asks us to do, He WILL give us the direction, strength, wisdom, and means to do it, as long as WE are yielded vessels.

Some weeks after God made it clear to me that I was to close my office, I was seeking Him in prayer one night and the Holy Spirit directed me to some Scripture in Genesis about Noah. I was confused about what it meant, so I asked, "Lord—What does anything about Noah have to do with ME?" Immediately the Holy Spirit began to speak as I wrote it down: "Just as I made a **covenant** with Noah, I have made one with you; just as I provided a **covering** for Noah, I have provided one for you; and just as Noah's **family** was with him, so your family will be with you!!"

A day or two later, the Holy Spirit directed me to a verse that I never remembered reading before. It was Psalm 25:14: "The secret [of the sweet, satisfying companionship] of the Lord have they who fear (revere and worship) Him, and **He will show them His covenant and reveal to them its [deep, inner] meaning.**" (Amplified, my emphasis) The Lord was gradually showing me what the covenant was that He wanted to make with me—it was the calling on my life! This new message I received from the Holy Spirit, together with this Scripture, gave me an awesome revelation that God was very serious about what He wanted me to do, and He wanted ME to take it seriously, too! Over time and in bits and pieces, He began showing me what the covenant, the covering, and the "family" business meant, and I don't think He's finished yet!

In the church service the following Sunday, the Holy Spirit directed me to share what He had told me with the congregation, because as He put it, "It was not just for you; it was also for this congregation!" He wanted His people in that Body to know that He has a covenant for EACH of their lives, and that He WILL make it known to them if they seek Him.

He made it clear that **the "covering" for us is both the anointing and the Blood**! Noah's "covering" involved both the physical and the spiritual. He had the spiritual aspect of the anointing of God, just as **we** do when we are operating in God's plan for our life. The anointing enabled him to carry out God's instructions concerning all the animals on the earth. What God asked him to do was a formidable human challenge; he could not have accomplished it without the anointing of God! The anointing gives us the love, power and wisdom to do what we could not humanly accomplish in the natural. Noah's physical "covering" was the ark itself, which protected him and his family, but at that point Jesus' Blood had not been shed in the Earth. **Today,**

the physical shedding of Jesus' Blood is our covering that protects us as we seek to carry out the direction of God for our lives!

I believe the part about Noah's family "being with him" was God's way of showing that His heart for the function of the family has never changed. Among the mighty things He is doing in the Earth at this time is a restoration to families; He has always wanted them to be in harmony, sharing in each others' goals and dreams. Noah's family had the collective favor and protection of God because of the righteousness of Noah himself. He was a spiritual leader and example to his family, which is what God still wants fathers to be….He is calling out to fathers in this generation to take their rightful position in the family!

The protection of Noah's family was a promise from God because of Noah's righteous life. We can also claim the numerous promises from God's Word that, as we obey the Lord and are in right standing with him, He will "bless the fruit of our womb," meaning our children. Psalm 112:1-2 promises: "Blessed is the man who fears the Lord, Who delights greatly in His commandments. His descendants will be mighty on earth; The generation of the upright will be blessed." (See also Deut. 7:13; Acts 2:38-39). The Book of Deuteronomy is full of admonitions to the people of Israel to teach the laws of God to their children so that they might live long lives and prosper.

God's design of the family is another means for Christians to prepare themselves to be the salt of the Earth! As Christian families pray together, serve God together, and show their love and commitment to each other, they set an example for the world to see—that God had some serious intentions for the "institution" of the family! Those intentions are about to be remarkably displayed again in the Earth as God restores the "prodigal" sons and daughters back to families, and raises up families to minister together, to the glory of God!!

As we pray and seek God, we need to be asking Him not only what He wants us to do as individuals, but what He wants to do in our families. Just as families have always been the foundation of our societies, God views families as the foundation of the local church. It is no accident that the Church Body is referred to as "the family of God," for in both the local churches and the Body of Christ worldwide, we must be an example of God's original intention for the **harmony of the family** in order to truly be the "salt" of the Earth.

Our relationships in the Body must first be **seasoned with love and maturity** in order to adequately "enhance" God's plan in the Earth. When we refer to someone as "seasoned" in a particular area of expertise or ability, we are referring to their maturity in that area. **God's intention was for us to become mature in the things of God so that we can truly be the "salt" that seasons our personal sphere of influence in the world and in the Body, His Church.**

Ephesians 4:11-14 explains "in a nutshell" why the spiritual gifts have been given to God's people: "And He Himself gave some to be apostles, some prophets, some evangelists, and some pastors and teachers, **for the equipping of the saints for the work of the ministry**, **for the edifying of the body of Christ**, till we all come to the unity of the faith and of the knowledge of the Son of God, to a perfect man, to the measure of the stature of the fullness of Christ; **that we should no longer be children tossed to and fro and carried about with every wind of doctrine**, by the trickery of men…."(My emphasis)

As mature Christians, we will not only be walking in the gifts and callings that God has revealed to us as our destiny, but we will be encouraging and building others up to do the same. In a mature body of Christ, there is no room for "competition"—envying or desiring others' gifts or "positions" amounts to denying God's plan for our OWN lives. In the self-confidence that comes with maturity, we will KNOW that the plan God has for us as individuals is special and unique, because WE are each special and unique!! Praise God for our own special blend of "seasoning salt" that is a unique recipe prepared for each believer!

CHAPTER 8

Overcoming Until the Wedding Day

As we go into the new Millenium, we are hearing and reading of many discussions and speculations by people in both the secular and the "religious" arenas concerning the events that are to come. Christians who believe that the events of the "end times" as described in the Bible are being fulfilled are being ridiculed for their belief. This should not surprise us, because I Corinthians 2:14 explains why this will take place: "But the natural man does not receive the things of the Spirit of God, for they are foolishness to him; nor can he know them, because they are spiritually discerned."

Those of us who have studied the Word of God, however, have a **hope** that the world doesn't have. It's that hope in being able to **overcome the world and Satan** that will keep the true believers steadfast until the day Jesus comes to take us to Heaven, or until we die! In Chapters 2 and 3 of the Book of Revelation, John the Revelator quotes the words of Jesus to the seven churches, which represent the seven church ages down through history. They are apparently also written to us today, however, because they point out the weaknesses in the Church that we can see even today. Jesus makes it clear that the churches who have an ear to listen and willingness to change can **overcome**. After each letter to an individual church, He gives a promise to that church that will be fulfilled **if they overcome**.

Obviously, Jesus would not tell us to do something that God did not give us the ability to do. In Romans 12:21, the Word COMMANDS us to overcome: "**Do not let yourself** be overcome by evil, but overcome (master) evil with good." (Amplified, my emphasis) Not only does the Word command us to overcome, but God EXPECTS us to overcome: "For this is the love of God, that we keep His commandments. And His commandments are not burdensome. For **whatever is born of God overcomes the world**. And this is the victory that has overcome the world—our faith. **Who is he who overcomes the world, but he who believes that Jesus is the Son of God**? This is He who came by water and blood—Jesus Christ...."(I John 5:3-6, my emphasis)

The Blood of Jesus is one of the greatest weapons we have with which to overcome Satan, **both now and in the days to come**, when Satan's powers will become even more evident in the world during the time of the Antichrist's reign and the Tribulation. Even though Revelation 12:10-11 refers to that time and to those who are left on Earth and accept Christ even after the Rapture, the application is for us now as well: "Then I heard a strong (loud) voice in heaven, saying, Now it has come—the salvation and the power and the kingdom (the dominion, the reign) of our God, and the power (the sovereignty, the authority) of His Christ (the Messiah); for the accuser of our brethren, he who keeps bringing before our God charges against them day and night, has been cast out! **And they have overcome**

(conquered) him by means of the blood of the Lamb and by the utterance of their testimony, for they did not love and cling to life even when faced with death [holding their lives cheap till they had to die for their witnessing]." (Amplified, my emphasis)

This Scripture confirms that those who believe in Christ have the power and authority to overcome Satan by trusting in the Blood of Jesus, which will give them power, boldness, and protection. They can also testify to their faith even in the midst of danger or threat, because even to die a physical death would be better than going to Hell for eternity. Those who truly know the Lord will be steadfast in this, and it will bring them the victory in the end!

I John 5:10-12 speaks of **the testimony of the believer**: "He who believes in the Son of God has the witness in himself; he who does not believe God has made Him a liar, because he has not believed the testimony that God has given of His Son. **And this is the testimony: that God has given us eternal life, and this life is in His Son. He who has the Son has life; he who does not have the Son of God does not have life.**" (My emphasis) This testimony is truly life-saving!

A further confirmation that this testimony is life-saving is at the end of the letter to Smyrna, where Jesus tells them: "He who **overcomes** shall not be hurt by the second death."(Rev.2:11, my emphasis) We know from Scripture that for some, there will be two deaths, a spiritual and a physical. Those who do not accept Christ will die physically, and then will burn eternally in the lake of fire, but **their spirits will die** because they will be eternally separated from God. Those who have experienced only one birth will have two deaths, but those who are "born again" (born twice) will die only once, and their spirits will live eternally.

Revelation 2:7 gives another promise for "overcomers": "To him who **overcomes** I will give to eat from the tree of life, which is in the midst of the Paradise of God." (My emphasis) This apparently refers back to the tree of life which Adam and Eve were told not to eat, because it would have given them immortality (see Genesis 3:22). But here God is confirming that His true followers WILL live eternally with Him in paradise!

"Overcoming" by the Blood of Jesus is the true testimony to the power of the Blood! I would like to review some specific aspects of overcoming by the Blood:

> 1) We must BELIEVE in it! The more we hear about it, study it, speak and sing about it, the more faith we will have in it! We must believe that **Satan has already been defeated by the Blood of Jesus**! If we believe in what the Blood has done for us, we will know that Satan **cannot defeat us** as children of God.
>
> 2) We must PLEAD the BLOOD of Jesus and avail ourselves of it every day, over every aspect of our lives, for protection against the plans of Satan. In doing this, we are recognizing and MAGNIFYING its importance in our lives! By doing this, we acknowledge Jesus as our "High Priest," and call upon Him as our Advocate and Intercessor!
>
> 3) We must CONFESS our sin daily and REPENT so that Satan cannot get a stronghold on us through the weaknesses of our flesh!
>
> 4) We must be in RIGHT RELATIONSHIP

with God AND with the Body of Christ. There is strength in the corporate anointing, oneness, and worship. The "wholeness" through the Blood should bring "wholeness" to the BODY, individually and corporately!

5) We must STAND on what the Word says about the Blood and what it has done for us! The Word of God is our "spiritual nourishment" that strengthens and fortifies us to stand against the temptations of the world and the attacks of the Enemy! It is a mighty "weapon," together with the Blood!

6) We must begin to MAGNIFY the Blood of Jesus, or "make much of it" and "esteem it highly" in our thought life, our prayer life and in our praise in order to see more of the power of God manifested through our lives!

The Word of God gives us a hope that we can't find in the world! It gives us the "**prescription**" for overcoming, the **authority** to overcome, and the **weapons** to use in overcoming. We have everything we need—it's up to us to be **willing and obedient!**

CHAPTER 9

Preparing for the Wedding Day: The Story of Esther and Haman

There are a number of Scriptures that refer to Christ as the "Bridegroom" and the Church as the "Bride," and passages referring to the "wedding Supper of the Lamb". In Matthew Chapter 25, the Parable of the Ten Virgins is an analogy to the prophetic day when Christ will come for His Bride, the Church, and implies that the Church must be "ready" when He comes. Only those who have the "oil," an analogy to the Holy Spirit, will be allowed to attend the wedding feast. In Matthew Chapter 22, the Parable of the Wedding Banquet tells the sad story of the wedding banquet the King prepared, but everyone he invited did not deserve to come. Verse 14 explains, "For many are called, (invited and summoned), but few are chosen." (Amplified)

Revelation 19:7 talks about the great day in Heaven when Jesus and the Church will "become one": "Let us be glad and rejoice and give him glory, for **the marriage of the Lamb has come, and His wife has made herself ready**." (My emphasis) When Jesus comes back to Earth, He and His Bride, the Church, will reign together! Revelation 3:21 confirms this in another promise to those who overcome: "**To him who overcomes**, I will grant to sit with Me on My throne, **as I also overcame** and sat down with My Father on His throne." (My emphasis)

These last Scriptures make it evident that **those who don't overcome** Satan and his influence in their lives **(by the power of the Blood, their testimony, and the help of the Holy Spirit), will never make it to the wedding day to sit down at the throne**! In preparing a teaching about "Overcoming by the Blood," I was unmistakably directed to the story of Esther and Haman in the Book of Esther. As I re-read it, it became increasingly clear to me that this story is a "type and shadow" of the future, **victorious** "Bride and Groom"—the Church and Christ—who will rule and reign in the Earth! Esther, the righteous, **overcame** Haman, the unrighteous, and earned the right to stay on the throne! She was also the **new bride** of the King!

It is no coincidence in this story that Esther was a Jew; she represents the final victory of the nation of Israel that will be won over all their enemies! Although she had to contend with some evil forces all around her, even in her own house—just as the people of Israel are contending with evil forces all around them today—she came out VICTORI-OUS—she OVERCAME!!

Esther Chapter 2 tells how King Ahasuerus went about finding himself a new bride, after banishing his former wife, Vashti, from his presence forever because she had refused his request for her to come to him. This in itself is actually a fore-shadowing of what will happen at the Great White Throne Judgment (see Revelation 20:11), when the unsaved will appear before God— those who have refused His invitation to come to Him. They, too, will be banished from the presence of the "King of Kings" forever, after their judgment takes place.

Esther Chapter 2 also describes the process by which the maidens went before the King for him to decide which one pleased him. When they went before the King, they were allowed to take anything with them that they wanted to in order to impress the King. Most of the women who went before him adorned themselves with ornaments, jewelry, plaited hair or luxurious fabrics. Esther revealed a **unique spirit,** however, in that she was not concerned about pleasing the King with her **outward** appearance. Chapter 2, verse 15, says: "Now when the turn for Esther the daughter of Abihail, the uncle of Mordecai who had taken her as his own daughter, had come to go in to the king, she required nothing but what Hegai the king's attendant, the keeper of the women, suggested. And Esther won favor in the sight of all who saw her." (Amplified)

Even though Esther knew nothing about the New Testament, she thoroughly fit the description of a perfect wife that Peter later gave in I Peter 3:3-4: "Let not yours be the [merely] external adorning with [elaborate] interweaving and knotting of the hair, the wearing of jewelry, or changes of clothes; but let it be the **inward adorning** and **beauty of the hidden person of the heart**, with the incorruptible and unfading charm of a gentle and peaceful spirit, which [is not anxious or wrought up, but] is very precious in the sight of God." (Amplified, my emphasis)

Esther chose NOT to put on any pretense—no false beauty or adornment—to go before the King—NOTHING FAKE!! She went with a sincere heart, wanting him to see her "inner beauty," and she won him over! Hebrews 10:22 says: "....let us draw near with a **true heart** in full assurance of faith...."(My emphasis) Esther went before the King in full assurance of faith that the King would see her **for** what she was—and God **allowed the King to see her heart so that he would choose Esther**.

This example speaks to us today of the reality that **God is setting apart** those who are coming to Him with a **pure heart! Hebrews 12:14 says that we should "Pursue peace with all people, and holiness, without which no one will see the Lord…."** We can be sure that God knows our hearts and that when judgment comes, **He will see people for what they are**! We can see this parallel to the example of Esther, the bride, as a warning to the Church today, for in it God is saying, "Woe to those who come before me ADORNED WITH DECEPTION!! They will NOT be a part of my CHOSEN BRIDE!"

This can be seen prophetically as a warning to the Church as a whole, but also to many pastors and Church leaders today who seem to have no revelation of the seriousness of this day and hour. The fire of God is about to consume and separate out of the Body those whose motivations are inconsistent with the heart of God! The extent to which greed, self-interest and pride have become a prime motivation for **some** pastors, evangelists and other Church leaders is a very sad reality. I truly believe that in these last days, God will no longer allow some of the things to continue in the Church that have been going on for years.

The most recent revelation I personally have received regarding this was a very serious and sobering prophetic word I received in my prayer time on January 20, 2003, which left me shaking and crying in intercession. The Holy Spirit spoke:

"I am coming with My wind to break the wills of many, even pastors. It won't be easy, but it will be pure and righteous and necessary for My Kingdom work. Many will submit, but some will not and will see My judgment! There IS a dividing line, which **no man** can separate; it is only by **My** hand that it is accomplished! There is a chasm in between, into which many will fall. Make no mistake about it—the separation has begun!

"My fire is coming to purge and to **make new**, those who would receive it. It is a serious thing, for it will determine the destinies of many who now think they are right with Me! The spirits of pride and control will be broken, or My judgment will come and **many will fall from the kingdoms they have established for themselves.**

"They must hear and heed My voice to escape the coming judgment! **There is much glory ahead for the Church for those who will hear and heed My warning.** I desire that **all** will heed and **all** will come, but they will not all come. The Glory will bring the Light the world needs. Manifest it wherever you go, and I will bless you and **all** those who will carry My Light! **It will be a glorious season for My Church, such as it has never seen. It is rapidly approaching—the fire and the rain will fall, to redeem and to restore many."**

Many will read this and say that this could not be from God, because He is a God of love. Yes, He is, but He is also a God of justice and judgment! One has only to read the Old Testament to verify that fact. And in the New Testament, **I Peter 4:17 says "For the time [has arrived] for judgment to begin with the household of God."** (Amplified, my emphasis)

A week after being given this word, I was having a discussion with my daughter about the "separation" the Holy Spirit spoke of, and I suddenly got a revelation that this word is a fulfillment of the prophecy in Revelation 3:15-16, where God is speaking to the Church in Laodicea, which many believe is symbolic of the church age of **today.** He says to them, "I know your [record of] works and what you are doing; you are neither cold nor hot. Would that you were cold or hot! So, **because you are lukewarm and neither cold nor hot, I will spew you out of My mouth!**" (My emphasis)

I suddenly realized why He said that....Because **the "lukewarms" are those who are walking the middle ground with God, with one foot in the world and one in God's Kingdom**. These people, who claim to be Christians but are still living like "the world" does, are a danger to the true witness of Christ in the world! There are also church leaders who live the same way and who are "forsaking the sheep" as described in Ezekiel Chapter 34, bearing false witness to the world! **Those** are the ones, with **one foot on either side of the "chasm,"** who will fall into it and be separated out, if they do not repent and turn around. Because they are disgusting to God, they will be "spewed out of His mouth."

In Romans 2:21-25, Paul addresses these types of people in the Church. Even though at the time he was speaking to the Jews, verses 28 and 29 reveal that we as Christians are really "spiritual Jews" because of the "circumcision of our hearts," so the warning applies to us today as well: **"You, therefore, who teach another, do you not teach yourself? You who preach that a man should not steal, do you steal? You who say, 'Do not commit adultery,' do you commit adultery? You who abhor idols, do you rob temples? You who make your boast in the law, do you dishonor God by breaking the law? For *'the name of God is blasphemed among the Gentiles because of you,'* as it is written."** (My emphasis)

Leaders must also begin to realize that, to deny or to squelch the calling of God on individual lives is to defy God Himself!! It is HIS plan that is being dishonored! We don't "equip the saints" for ministry simply by preaching to people, or by teaching them the Word of God. We equip them by also **giving people the encouragement and the opportunity to operate in the spiritual gifts they have been given, and by nurturing them and mentoring them in those gifts**. It is obvious from New Testament Scripture that people in the church were freely given the opportunity to operate in their spiritual giftings in the church, as long as they were "in order." Leaders who deny or suppress the gifts and the calling in others' lives are in reality denying the **G**race of God, the **A**nointing of God, and the **P**eople of God. Notice there's a "GAP" there!! Any place that this occurs, there is definitely "something missing" from the fullness God wants the Church and His people to walk in in this hour! I believe that Church leaders will be held accountable for their part in subjugating God's plan.

The good news is that God is merciful and wants to cleanse, forgive, and restore His people! Anyone who calls on the name of the Lord and is willing to humble himself, seek the Lord's face, and repent, He WILL restore. Again, it is God's kindness that is intended to lead us to repentance! In the coming "tidal wave" of God's Spirit that will be poured out in the Earth, many will be purged, restored, and brought back into right fellowship with God and His people. **"He who has an ear, let him hear what the Spirit says to the churches."** (Rev. 3:22, my emphasis)

The story of Esther also tells us in Chapter 2, verse 12, that there was a preparation time of purification which had to take place BEFORE the maidens could go to the King: "Each young woman's turn came to go in to King Ahasuerus after she had completed twelve months' preparation, according to the regulations for the women, for thus were the days of their preparation apportioned: six months with oil of **myrrh**, and six months with **perfumes** for beautifying women." (My emphasis)

So myrrh was the first thing that was used for a period of six months. Myrrh is an herbal medicine that is excellent for **cleansing and healing**, and is very good for **healing sores and wounds**. It is also antiseptic—it **gets rid of infection**. It helps to **remove toxic waste from the body**, and it gives **strength and vitality.**

Esther's purification time using myrrh is a foreshadowing of the **purification** that the Body of Christ is now going through! God is putting us through a **cleansing and healing process**—getting rid of the "spots and wounds" so that we can be presented to Him as the perfect Bride! **He is separating out the "infectious stuff" that is trying to invade the Body of Christ** and keep it from its destiny with God. He's separating out the "toxic" elements, in order to give strength and vitality to the Body! Ephesians 5:25-27 tells us God's plan for purification of the Body of Christ: "Husbands, love your wives, just as Christ also loved the church and gave Himself for her, that He might **sanctify and cleanse** her with the washing of water by the word, that He might present her to Himself a glorious church, **not having spot or wrinkle** or any such thing, but that **she should be holy and without blemish**." (My emphasis)

Right at this time in history, many people are responding to God's Spirit calling upon them to be **holy—set apart for God—and committed to fulfilling His plan in the Earth.** After the "purification" process is complete, when all the "stains and wrinkles" are gone, we will stand at the threshold, ready to meet our Bridegroom, and **our purity will be the perfume that adorns us**, making us a "sweet fragrance" to Him! This completes the analogy to the second six months of the maiden's preparation time using perfumes and cosmetics!

In Revelation 19:6-8, we read about the "fine linen," or the "wedding gown" of the Church, which represents the righteous life and holy conduct of God's committed people. Our righteousness and holiness will ADORN our wedding dress, so that when we're presented to Jesus, **we'll be beautiful in His eyes!** Matthew 22:11-14 tells about those who will be turned away, however, because they don't have a proper "wedding dress." Our wedding gown will be used only once—to get us into the wedding—but throughout eternity, the righteousness and holiness **of Jesus** will "clothe" us!!

Notice that Esther could not be called the "bride" until she waited for **the appointed time**. We as the Church body also must endure until the "purification" process is complete—and until the **appointed time for Jesus to return** for His Bride! The Body of Christ is now in the process of becoming the "spotless Bride"....the Holy Spirit is teaching us to walk in obedience, spiritual maturity, wholeness of body, soul and spirit, and in **holiness.**

In Chapter 4, Esther made the decision to go before the King unannounced, knowing it was a dangerous thing to do. She knew she could have been put to death, because it was against the law. But God spoke through Mordecai to her, and she knew she had to intercede for her people. She declared, "....and if I perish, I perish." (Esther 4:16) **In order to overcome in these last days,** the people of God must have the same resolve— to do the will of God and listen to God's voice, even if it means endangering ourselves. When we show God that we are **willing and obedient**, He will then, through the Blood of Jesus, give us protection, as He protected Esther!

The point is, that **just as WE would have no right to go before God if it weren't for our righteousness through the Blood of Jesus and the mercy of God**, (the "King of Kings"), Esther's righteousness and the King's mercy allowed her to go in UNHARMED! But also—**she was favored by God and protected because she yielded herself to the plan of God!** This was evidenced, too, by her willingness to submit herself to a three-day fast and to ask others to do the same. The King was **merciful** to Esther, just as God is merciful to us! Esther **trusted in his mercy and his love for her,** or she would not have gone before him. We must also trust in the love and the mercy of God, because those things will never fail us. **The Blood itself is truly a "manifestation of God's love," poured out for all the**

world to see and experience!!

The glimpses of Mordecai's faithfulness to God that we see in this story have great applications for us in this day and time as well. In Chapter 5, verse 9, Haman became furious because Mordecai refused to rise when he walked by or to show "fear" in his presence. Mordecai refused to pay homage to Haman because he looked it at as an affront to the sovereignty of Jehovah God. His loyalty to God would not allow him to bow down to another human being. Besides that, Haman WAS an IDOLATOR—he idolized himself, his power, his position, and his money! We see that God protected Mordecai and rewarded him in the end for his refusal to pay homage to someone other than God.

In these last days, there will be MANY false teachers, false prophets, and false idols, but God Almighty is going to protect and reward those of us who resist bowing our knee to them! II Peter Chapter 2 talks about "false teachers and their destruction," but verses 9 and 10 tell us, **"....the Lord knows how to deliver the godly out of temptations and to reserve the unjust under punishment for the day of judgment, and especially those who walk according to the flesh in the lust of uncleanness and despise authority."** (My emphasis)

In Esther 8:7, the King says to Esther and Mordecai: "Behold, I have given Esther the house of Haman, and him they have hanged upon the gallows because he laid his hand upon the Jews." (Amplified) This statement also signifies what is going to take place soon in the Earth! Those who come against the nation of Israel and Jehovah God are not only going to suffer defeat and death, "But the wealth of the sinner is stored up for the righteous"! (Prov.13:22)

In Isaiah 23, a chapter entitled "A Prophecy About Tyre," we see another allusion in verse 18 to a great transfer of wealth from the merchants of the world into the hands of the children of God: "**But her gain and her hire** [the profits of Tyre's new prosperity] will be dedicated to the Lord [eventually]; it **will not be treasured or stored up, for her gain will be used for those who dwell in the presence of the Lord [the ministers],** that they may eat sufficiently and have durable and stately clothing [suitable for those who minister at God's altar]."(Amplified, my emphasis) The prosperity that many believe will supernaturally be transferred into the hands of Christians in these last days will be mainly for the purpose of supplying the great financial needs in getting the Gospel to every nation and people on Earth. There will be a tremendous harvest of souls into God's kingdom before our Lord's return!

In Chapter 8 of the Book of Esther, King Ahasuerus explained to Esther that he could not "undo" the edict that had been written by Haman and sealed by the King, allowing for the destruction of the Jews in all of the King's provinces. What he did do, however, to please Esther and Mordecai, was to write another decree giving the Jews the right to "gather and defend their lives; to destroy, to slay, and to wipe out any armed force that might attack them, their little ones, and women; and to take the enemies' goods for spoil." (Esther 8:11, Amplified) The King **sealed** the decree with his ring, **allowing the Jews to overcome their enemies.** The Blood of Jesus has **sealed our covenant** with the King of Kings, which now gives us as Christians ("spiritual Jews" according to Rom. 2:29), **the power to overcome OUR enemies!**

The last verse of the Book of Esther says that "….Mordecai the Jew was next to King Ahasuerus and great among the Jews, and was a favorite with the multitude of his brethren, for he sought the welfare of his people and spoke peace to his whole race." (Amplified) What a "turnaround" that was for Mordecai! I believe that God is getting ready to do a "supernatural turnaround," not only for the Jews, but for all those who have stood up for their welfare! We will be seeing more and more Jewish people come into a revelation of the fulfillment of prophecy in the life of Jesus. More and more will receive the revelation of what the Blood of Jesus has done for them, as well as for the Gentiles. They will begin to understand and receive Romans 1:16, which declares: "For I am not ashamed of the gospel of Christ, for it is the power of God to salvation for everyone who believes, **for the Jew first and also for the Greek."** (My emphasis)

As we magnify the Blood of Jesus and take hold of the power that is available to us, the signs and wonders that result will draw men to the Light! Isaiah 55:5-6 speaks of a time when **men of all nations will run to the anointing**, because they have seen the glory of God on His people: "Surely you shall call a nation you do not know, And nations who do not know you shall run to you, Because of the Lord your God, and the Holy One of Israel; For He has glorified you." **In this time of the great harvest of souls, thousands around the world are being added daily to the Body of the Bride of Christ, and are being prepared physically, emotionally and spiritually to be welcomed by the Bridegroom, Jesus Himself!**

As we remain steadfast in overcoming until that glorious Wedding Day, we will be the "Light-bearers" who reflect His Glory! When we magnify the blood in the natural, we can see much more clearly how it is working in the human body. When we begin to magnify the Blood of Jesus and to esteem it highly, we will see more clearly how it is working in our lives, and in the Body of Christ. In MAGNIFYING the Blood, we WILL see the Glory of God, manifested through our individual lives, and through the Body of Christ corporately, **for that has always been the plan of God! Whether or not the world believes it, recognizes it, or acknowledges it, the glory of God IS BEING—and will continue to be—revealed more and more through us, His**

creation! We are truly carrying about in our bodies the dying of the Lord Jesus, so that the life of Jesus also may be manifested in our bodies, and in the Body of Christ! To God be all the Glory, for all He has ordained and accomplished through the precious Blood of Jesus!!

Notes

Chapter One

1. Williams, Jimmy (General ed.): *Evidence, Answers, and Christian Faith*, (Grand Rapids, MI: Kregel Publications, 2002), p. 87.
2. Ibid., p. 89.
3. Ibid., p. 91.

Chapter Two

1. *Alternative Medicine, the Definitive Guide* (Puyallup, WA.: Future Medicine Publishing, Inc., 1994), p.282.

Chapter Four

1. *The Wycliffe Bible Commentary,* Charles F. Pfeiffer and Everett F. Harrison, (Chicago, IL: Moody Press, 1962), p. 652.

Chapter Five

1. Schlossberg, Leon and Zuidema, George D., M.D., (ed.): *The Johns Hopkins Atlas of Human Functional Anatomy, third ed.,* p.26. © 1986 Reprinted with permission of the Johns Hopkins University Press.
2. Roach, Mary, 'Can You Laugh Your Stress Away?', *Health*, Sept.1996, pp.94-95.

Chapter Six

1. Dr. M. Ted Morter, Jr., *Your Health Your Choice* (Hollywood, FL.: LifetimeBooks, Inc.,1992), p.54.
2. Ibid., p.57.
3. Ibid., p.58.
4. Ibid., p.61.
5. By permission. From *Merriam-Webster Online Dictionary* © *2003* by Merriam-Webster, Incorporated (www.Merriam-Webster.com).
6. Ibid.
7. Ibid.

Chapter Seven

1. *World Book Encyclopedia* (Chicago, IL: Field Enterprises Educational Corporation, 1972), Vol.17, p.68.
2. Ibid., p.70.
3. Source is adapted from Venes, D. J. (ed.): *Taber's Cyclopedic Medical Dictionary,* ed. 19, F. A. Davis, Philadelphia, 2001.
4. Ibid.
5. *World Book,* p. 72.

6. *Taber's.*
7. Ibid.

CPSIA information can be obtained
at www.ICGtesting.com
Printed in the USA
LVHW091410121021
700235LV00005B/202

9 781594 674976